STARTING TO COLLECT SERIES

ANTIQUE SILVER

Ian Pickford

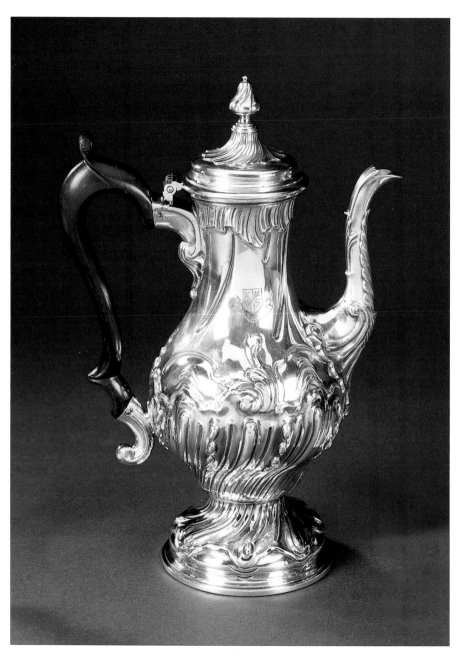

Coffee pot made in London by Alexander Johnston in 1761.

Sotheby's

STARTING TO COLLECT SERIES

ANTIQUE SILVER

Ian Pickford

WITHDRAWN

ANTIQUE COLLECTORS' CLUB

Printed in England
by the Antique Collectors' Club Ltd., Old Martlesham, Woodbridge, Suffolk
on Consort Royal Era Satin paper
supplied by the Donside Paper Company, Aberdeen, Scotland

The Antique Collectors' Club

The Antique Collectors' Club was formed in 1966 and quickly grew to a five figure membership spread throughout the world. It publishes the only independently run monthly antiques magazine, *Antique Collecting*, which caters for those collectors who are interested in widening their knowledge of antiques, both by greater awareness of quality and by discussion of the factors which influence the price that is likely to be asked. The Antique Collectors' Club pioneered the provision of information on prices for collectors and the magazine still leads in the provision of detailed articles on a variety of subjects.

It was in response to the enormous demand for information on 'what to pay' that the price guide series was introduced in 1968 with the first edition of *The Price Guide to Antique Furniture* (completely revised 1978 and 1989), a book which broke new ground by illustrating the more common types of antique furniture, the sort that collectors could buy in shops and at auctions rather than the rare museum pieces which had previously been used (and still to a large extent are used) to make up the limited amount of illustrations in books published by commercial publishers. Many other price guides have followed, all copiously illustrated, and greatly appreciated by collectors for the valuable information they contain, quite apart from prices. The Price Guide Series heralded the publication of many standard works of reference on art and antiques. *The Dictionary of British Art* (now in six volumes), *The Pictorial Dictionary of British 19th Century Furniture Design, Oak Furniture* and *Early English Clocks* were followed by many deeply researched reference works such as *The Directory of Gold and Silversmiths*, providing new information. Many of these books are now accepted as the standard work of reference on their subject.

The Antique Collectors' Club has widened its list to include books on gardens and architecture. All the Club's publications are available through bookshops world wide and a full catalogue of all these titles is available free of charge from the addresses below.

Club membership, open to all collectors, costs little. Members receive free of charge *Antique Collecting*, the Club's magazine (published ten times a year), which contains well-illustrated articles dealing with the practical aspects of collecting not normally dealt with by magazines. Prices, features of value, investment potential, fakes and forgeries are all given prominence in the magazine.

Among other facilities available to members are private buying and selling facilities and the opportunity to meet other collectors at their local antique collectors' clubs. There are over eighty in Britain and more than a dozen overseas. Members may also buy the Club's publications at special pre-publication prices.

As its motto implies, the Club is an organisation designed to help collectors get the most out of their hobby: it is informal and friendly and gives enormous enjoyment to all concerned.

For Collectors — By Collectors — About Collecting

ANTIQUE COLLECTORS' CLUB
Sandy Lane, Old Martlesham, Woodbridge, Suffolk, IP12 4SD, UK
Tel: (01394) 389950 Fax: (01394) 389999
Email: sales@antique-acc.com Website: www.antique-acc.com
———————— *or* ————————
Market Street Industrial Park, Wappingers' Falls, NY 12590, USA
Tel: 845 297 0003 Fax: 845 297 0068
Email: info@antiquecc.com Website: www.antiquecc.com

To Adrian and Sophia

Acknowledgements

The author would like to express his thanks to all those who have assisted in various ways with this book.

In particular The Wardens of the Goldsmiths Company; David Beasley, Librarian of the Goldsmiths Company; Victoria Lane, Assistant Librarian of the Goldsmiths Company; and in the Assay Office of Goldsmiths Hall – David Evans, Deputy Warden; Paul Johnson, Superintendant Assayer; and Geraldine Mitchell, the Assay Master's Secretary.

For assistance with photographs and photography I should like to thank Asprey & Co. Ltd., Bonhams, Christie's New York, Christie's South Kensington, Michael McAleer, Phillips the International Fine Art Auctioneers, and Sotheby's.

I should like to thank the following individuals – Alexis Butcher, Eileen Goodway, Christopher Hartop, Rupert Slingsby, and Peter Waldron. In addition my grateful thanks go to the private individuals who have lent objects to be photographed from their collections but who wish to remain anonymous.

My thanks also go to Primrose Elliott, my Editor, and all those involved in the production of this work at the Antique Collectors' Club.

Finally I should like to thank Linda, my wife, for all her support, and secretarial help, during the writing of this book.

Contents

Introduction

The aim of this book is to introduce new collectors and enthusiasts to the marvellous subject of silver. I have done this by going step by step through various aspects of the subject, starting with the material itself, going on to the marking system and then to how silver is made.

A knowledge of silversmithing techniques is very important to an understanding of the subject. Without this technical expressions would be meaningless 'jargon' and quite daunting. The most important techniques involved in making and decorating silver are therefore explained.

Having looked at some of the famous English makers I have gone on to cover the areas most favoured by collectors and those wishing to purchase silver simply for use. It has been a deliberate policy not to include objects outside the normal collecting spheres except where they may be of importance to illustrate a particular point or development. Livery pots, medieval mazers and Tudor principal salts will therefore not be found in these pages whereas spoons, snuff boxes and pincushions will.

An area of collecting which has often been misunderstood is that of plating. The problems of distinguishing the various types has frequently led to its avoidance by potential collectors. This is a pity since it is a most fascinating and rewarding area. The chapter which I have included on this subject will I hope help to make it easier to understand.

Anyone embarking on collecting silver needs to know how to look after their pieces so this is covered as well as pointers on how to avoid some of the pitfalls.

Finally I have given some ideas about buying, further reading, important collections and various clubs as well as courses that may be of interest to those wishing to extend their knowledge further.

CHAPTER 1

Why Silver?

Silver is a remarkable metal with some extraordinary properties. To understand it fully it is a good idea to start by being aware of these and where the metal itself comes from.

It is one of the earliest metals to have been used by man (from the 3rd millennium BC), requiring only simple technology to extract it from its ores. On rare occasions it may even be found as native silver (the metal itself, not as an ore).

The ancient Greeks exploited the rich deposits of silver to be found in and around Athens. It was the discovery of a new seam which paid for a new fleet, saving the Greeks from defeat and, arguably, as a result, saving civilisation.

Apart from Greece (Carpathea), other early sources of precious metal were Iberia and Britain (a particularly important source of gold in prehistoric times).

Although silver is found in Britain (to the west of the Pennines), much was accumulated as a result of international trading – first the export of grain and subsequently wool – which was most usually paid for in silver and gold. There were even laws (from the end of the thirteenth century) prohibiting the export of silver from England. So much was accumulated that the 'vast quantity of curiously and marvelously wrought silver' to be found in England was often commented upon by foreign visitors.

The sixteenth century saw the discovery in Spanish America of new sources. Vast quantities were brought back by the Spaniards, much of which was diverted by Drake and a few others to England. So much was brought in that the price of bullion[1] fell.

During the nineteenth century huge new deposits were discovered in North America, Mexico and Australia. Spanish America continues to be a major source of new silver with Mexico being today one of the few countries mining silver as silver rather than obtaining it as a by-product of copper or lead mining. As a result of all the new deposits that have been found, the value of silver today per ounce is in real terms far less than it has ever been in the past.

Silver is one of the most malleable and ductile of all materials. In other words it can be beaten out into sheets and drawn out into wire with ease – in the case of the former to the thinnest of leaves and the latter to wires so thin that a powerful microscope is required even to see them. One Troy ounce[2] of silver may be drawn out into a wire over forty miles long!

The properties of silver mean that a craftsman may work it into virtually any shape or form that his imagination can create. Silver is almost limitless in its ability to be formed. Once a shape or form has been produced it will retain this for all time unless something fairly radical is done to it.

If one adds to the above the fact that silver, when polished, reflects light better than any other material known to man, it is easy to see why it has appealed to artists and craftsmen over the centuries.

Other interesting properties include it being the finest conductor of both heat and electricity that there is. It is also self-sterilising; bacteria cannot survive on its surface. This led to its being used over many centuries for medical instruments. Although not understanding why, early medical men had obviously found by experience that fewer patients died if silver instruments were used. The introduction of both the NHS and modern sterilising methods led to the decline of its use in medicine. Today antique silver medical instruments are very collectable.

One of the biggest users of silver until recently has been the photographic industry. This was developed from the discovery of the light sensitivity of certain silver compounds such as silver bromide (the old bromide paper). Until Bunker Hunt[3] forced the price of silver to an all time high, the photographic industry was content to carry on using large quantities for everything from holiday snaps to X-rays.

The move away from silver by the photographic industry turned a world under-production into a world over-production with naturally a resultant drop in price.

The word silver itself derives from the Anglo Saxon *seolfer* and has the unique distinction of being the only word in the English language for which there is no rhyme. Its chemical symbol Ag derives from the earlier Latin *argentium* from which the French word *argent* comes.

Silver is placed with gold and copper in the same chemical group (periodic table IB). All three have similar properties and are frequently found together in nature as well as being combined together by man.

Good examples of the latter are silver gilt – silver 'covered' with a thin layer of gold – and Old Sheffield plate – copper with a thin layer of silver fused to the surface.

Comparisons with gold and copper are useful, since they illustrate well why it is silver, rather than the other two, which has found greatest favour with the artist-craftsman over the years.

The great disadvantage with gold is not its high cost, which many over the centuries have been well able to afford, but its weight. Gold, after platinum, is the heaviest substance known to man. Volume for volume it is about half as heavy again as silver, and lead. As a result a coffee pot which in silver weighs, say, 30oz. would if made to the same specifications in gold weigh about 45oz. Whereas the former is comfortable, the latter is cumbersome. It is not therefore surprising that the use of gold is normally confined to small objects – jewellery, objects of vertu etc. – and thus when something larger is required it is made of silver

covered with gold (silver gilt). There are in fact less than one hundred known pieces of antique English gold in the form of larger objects – cups, candlesticks, teapots etc.

With copper the problem lies not in its weight but in two other respects. The first is technical. You cannot cast[4] copper in a normal atmosphere. This is why copper kettles, pans, etc. have their cast parts made of brass.

The second problem is that verdigris (green spots) form on copper. Not only is this unsightly but it is also very poisonous. This is why copper cooking utensils should always have tinned interiors (except jam pans – the temperature required to make jam is higher than the melting point of tin).

Therefore, to make an object in copper will often require the introduction of two other metals – brass and tin. If you were to compare all other metals with silver all would be found wanting in some respect. Some metals are easier to work than silver. Lead, for example, is certainly very workable, but just about everything else is wrong with it. It melts at 327°C, the temperature of a moderate oven (silver melts at 960.5°C). It also, even at normal temperatures, will not hold its shape; look at old lead piping. Food and liquids consumed from it would poison you and, finally, just try polishing it.

Other metals go to the opposite extreme. Try working iron or steel in a cold state.

Such problems as exist with silver are for the most part easily overcome. As already mentioned, it is the finest conductor of heat known. It is for this reason that the handles of teapots etc. are usually made of wood (modern ones may be fibre or even plastic). When a silver handle is used, insulators, generally made of ivory, will be found.

---

1. Bullion. Silver or gold in its raw state (i.e. before manufacturing or coining).

2. Troy ounces are used to weigh precious metals (1 Troy ounce = 31.1 grams).

3. From August 1979 to March 1980 Bunker Hunt, with others, attempted to corner the world silver market. At its peak silver rose to just over £20 per Troy ounce.

4. See page 33.

Why Silver Marking?

In its pure state silver is a little too soft to be practical for either coinage or for domestic and ceremonial use. It was found that by adding small quantities of copper it became significantly harder and more durable. Thus Greek and Roman silver, when discovered, is a mixture of these two metals.

During the Saxon period in England the percentage of silver in the pennies produced was fixed at a minimum 92.5% silver (the other 7.5% being copper). This alloy gave sufficient strength whilst retaining a high intrinsic value and good colour.

The connection between the coinage and the domestic silver of England was of great importance until comparatively recent times. One of the principal ways in which a man could store his wealth was in objects of silver. During prosperous times objects would be commissioned from the goldsmiths. However, fortunes fluctuated and in bad times these would be taken to the nearest mint to be melted and coined. Perhaps a hundred years later these coins would in turn be melted to produce cups or spoons. With this continuous conversion of silver from domestic use to currency and vice versa certain problems could easily arise.

The coinage had to be of a set standard. Imagine what would have happened if the domestic and, for that matter, ecclesiastic silver had been of either a different standard or of no fixed standard at all. The mints would then have had to refine every piece submitted for coining. The standard for coins and for goldsmiths' work was therefore made the same. The ordinance of 1238 states that no goldsmiths should use any silver worse than the standard of the coin, i.e. 92.5% minimum silver content.

Having established such standards, how then was it possible to enforce them and how was it possible to determine the standard of silver in an existing object?

Enforcement was achieved by appointing wardens who under the same ordinance of 1238 had the power to search out and bring to justice any offenders.

The testing, assessing or assaying of silver was at this early period carried out using a black stone with a matt surface known as a touch stone on which the silver to be tested was rubbed. The colour of metal on the block was then observed, and compared with a known standard, from which the quality was determined. If the smear from the piece being tested was the same colour or whiter than the sample of known standard, then all was well. If 'yellower' then it was below standard and the piece would be destroyed.

During the twelfth century, due to their international reputation for their skills of refining and testing silver together with their honesty, certain individuals from the Baltic area were offered posts by the English crown controlling the standards of the coinage. It is believed that as a result of their coming from the East they were known in England as the Easterlings. Since they were controlling the standard of coin this was then probably known as the Easterlings, or Esterlings, Standard which in later years was corrupted to Sterling – hence our modern word for standard silver.

With the improvements of silver standards in England by the second half of the thirteenth century certain new problems were encountered. These were basically that sub-standard continental coins such as Pollards and Crockards together with goldsmiths' work were being exchanged weight for weight with English sterling standard silver. To stop this drain on English national wealth King Edward I passed the 'Statutum de Moneta' by which the import and circulation of foreign coins was forbidden. In addition, a licence from the King was necessary before anyone could take any piece of silver out of the realm. In 1300 the Constable of Dover Castle was ordered 'not to permit any silver money or any other white money of the King's mint or any other mint, or any silver vessels, or any silver in mass or in any other way to be taken to ports beyond the sea without the King's special licence, under pain of forfeiture of life and goods'. This had also to be read at all the ports in England every fifteen days. Despite such strict controls several merchants, particularly those of Flanders, still attempted to take silver out of the realm 'secretly in sacks of wool, hides, bales and otherwise in divers manners', and import base coinage.

Licences to take silver 'beyond seas' were not easy to obtain. In 1302 the Prior of Holy Trinity, York, was permitted to cross from Dover 'provided he has no money or silver with him'. The Master of the Temple and the Elect of York managed to obtain licences, in the case of the latter for up to £100 for expenses. The Archbishop of Canterbury when going abroad in 1306 was reminded of the King's ordinance and ordered not to take money etc., in mass out of the realm.

It is when taken in context with their earlier enactments and ordinances that the reasons for the important Act of King Edward I which became law in 1300 can be best understood. This was of course the Act requiring the leopard's head to be struck on English silver and gold which had been assayed and passed by the wardens of the craft. As a result of this Act it was possible for officials at ports readily to identify English silver. Subsequently mints could immediately know whether an object presented to them for coining was of the correct standard. But above all it meant that the standards of the goldsmiths throughout the realm could be more closely controlled. Thus started what is perhaps the oldest form of consumer protection – the hallmark.

CHAPTER 3

Understanding Hallmarks

The best way to understand a hallmark is to know why each mark was added to the system. It is also best to get to know the marks of London first; provincial marking should then be much easier to understand.

The leopard's head which, just to confuse, should actually be a lion's head from the French heraldic *leo*pard, was, as we have seen above, introduced in 1300. It was not peculiar to London but was the King's mark for use throughout the country on both gold and silver.

This should have been the only mark required and might well have been had there not been some unscrupulous goldsmiths. These men made their own leopard's head punches which they then stamped on sub-standard pieces, passing them on to an unsuspecting public.

When it was realised what was going on (it started to affect the coinage), a new mark was in 1363 introduced – the maker's mark. This enabled the authorities to identify the person responsible for any piece found to have a fraudulent leopard's head.

Early makers' marks were symbols. With the spread of literacy from the end of the fifteenth century onwards initials gradually appeared, often combined with symbols. By the late eighteenth century initials had taken over almost completely. Today the maker's mark is officially described as a sponsor's mark.

For just over one hundred years after 1363 two marks should be found on any piece of silver or gold – the leopard's head and maker's mark. Having said this, however, it is clear from the extremely rare surviving pieces from this period that not everything was marked.

The next addition to the system was in 1478 with the introduction of what is known today as the date letter. Its introduction was due to the dishonesty of the touch wardens. These were the officials who, up to this date, had tested silver and gold in London. The problem arose because the testing was carried out in the goldsmiths' own shops. As a result of this these men were more easily open to corruption, and were stamping the official leopard's head on sub-standard silver. This had become such a problem that it affected the coinage, the Mint naturally accepting any officially marked piece as being of the correct standard, and then turning it into coin.

To curb this the system was changed. From 1478 onwards pieces had to be taken to an office (the Assay Office) in Goldsmiths' Hall, hence hallmarking. There the piece could be tested and, if up to standard, marked under the watchful eye of the Assay Master.

To ensure the honesty of the Assay Master who was appointed in May (the start of the goldsmiths' year) for a year, he was given a mark for that year by which he could be identified. The mark chosen was a letter of the alphabet. This started with an A in 1478 and moved on through twenty letters of the alphabet. A new cycle was then commenced using a different style of alphabet. This happened regardless of whether the same man was reappointed or not. Coincidentally, this has meant that from 1478 onwards precise dating to a year has been possible.

Today the date letter does represent exactly that and since 1975 has been a calendar year. Up to 1975 you will find in hallmark books that the year is given as, for example, 1757/8. This is due to the year starting in May. When, however, an object is described or catalogued, the date is normally given as 1757.

From 1478 until 1544 three marks should be struck – leopard's head (which acquired a crown in 1478), maker's mark, and date letter.

In 1544 Henry VIII took over the Assay Office. To show royal control a fourth mark was added – the lion passant. This, probably the most famous mark to be found on English silver, is often referred to as 'The Sterling Lion', representing as it does today not royal control (which ceased in 1549) but sterling standard.

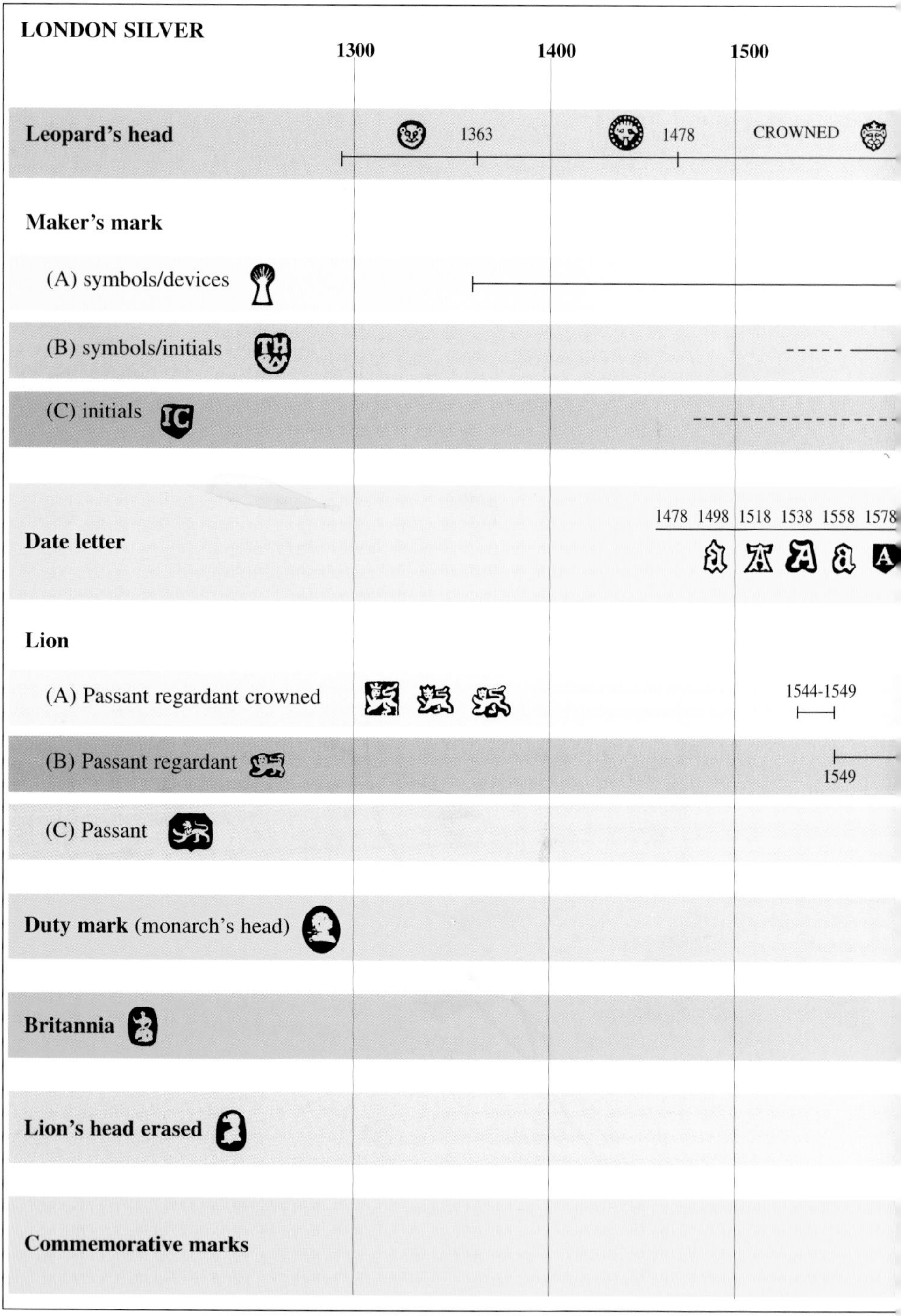

LONDON SILVER

	1300	1400	1500

Leopard's head — 1363, 1478, CROWNED

Maker's mark

(A) symbols/devices

(B) symbols/initials

(C) initials

Date letter

1478 1498 1518 1538 1558 1578

Lion

(A) Passant regardant crowned — 1544-1549

(B) Passant regardant — 1549

(C) Passant

Duty mark (monarch's head)

Britannia

Lion's head erased

Commemorative marks

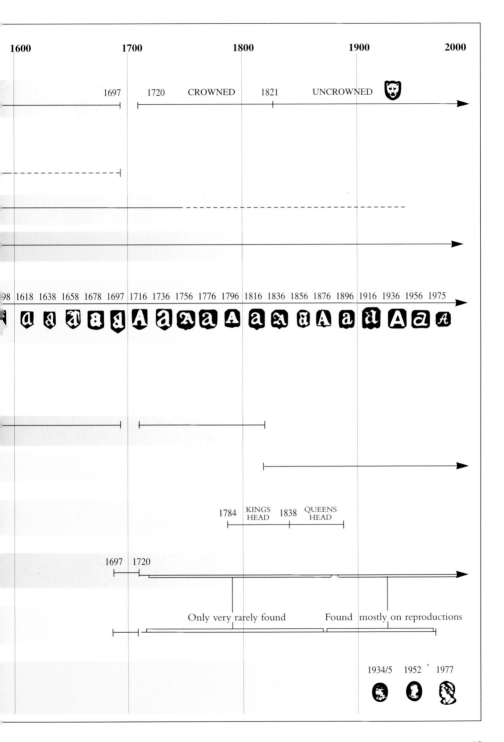

1600   1700   1800   1900   2000

1697   1720   CROWNED   1821   UNCROWNED

98 1618 1638 1658 1678 1697 1716 1736 1756 1776 1796 1816 1836 1856 1876 1896 1916 1936 1956 1975

1784   KINGS HEAD   1838   QUEENS HEAD

1697   1720

Only very rarely found   Found mostly on reproductions

1934/5   1952   1977

15

What may be regarded as the established system of four marks – leopard's head, maker's mark, date letter and lion passant was thus in operation from 1544 onwards.

At the end of the seventeenth century there was a hiccup in the system resulting from the introduction in 1697 of a higher standard, known as Britannia Standard. The increase in purity was from a minimum 92.5% to 95.84%. This made it much more difficult for the goldsmiths to use the coinage as their source of silver and effectively stopped the wholesale destruction of the coinage which had been going on.

To show that this new standard was in force all the marks were changed. The figure of Britannia replaced the sterling lion (hence Britannia Standard), and the lion's head erased (erased is a heraldic term meaning cut off) replaced the leopard's head. A new cycle of date letters was also started (a year earlier than normal) and all makers had to register a new maker's mark representing the first two letters of their surname rather than their initials which had formerly been the norm. Gold was not affected by these changes.

In 1720 Sterling was reintroduced using the same form of marking as before. From 1720 up to the present day the two standards Sterling and Britannia have run parallel. Effectively the use of Britannia Standard died out very quickly after 1720 and is found only rarely after the mid-1730s until its revival in the late nineteenth century. Today it accounts for only a tiny percentage of the silver passing through the London Assay Office.

To help curb possible fraudulent practices the lion's head erased has not been used from 1975 onwards (the normal leopard's head replaces it).

In 1784, to pay for the American War of Independence, duty was imposed on silver. To show that it had been paid a new mark was introduced – the monarch's head. It took a long time to pay for this war, the heads of successive monarchs being marked on English silver up to 1890.

Monarchs' heads may be found after 1890 – the first of these in 1934-5 (Jubilee), the next in 1952-3 (Coronation) and the most recent in 1977 (Jubilee). These are however voluntary additional marks, commemorating events, and not true hallmarks.

During the period of the duty mark 1784-1890 and in the years of commemorative marks five marks will be found – leopard's head, maker's mark, date letter, lion passant and monarch's head.

Having looked at the development of the system there are one or two further points which are worth remembering.

The year 1821 in London saw two significant changes. There is as yet no satisfactory explanation as to why these happened but they did and they are useful.

The first is that the leopard's head lost its crown and the second is that the lion passant which had been gardant (looking out at you) now looked straight ahead (to the left). If the mark is at all worn it is probably the leopard's head which will be easiest to distinguish (crowned or uncrowned).

A table is perhaps useful (and is given on pages 14 and 15) since with this it should be possible to narrow down very quickly the period of a mark. As an example:

Both the above have a similar date letter and very similar duty marks which, taken on their own, could be difficult and confusing.

In both cases the duty mark narrows the period down to between 1784 and 1890 – being a king's head duty mark puts both pieces between 1784 and 1837. (In 1837 Queen Victoria's head was used for the first time and continued to 1890.)

The crowned leopard's head puts the first mark before 1821 and the lack of crown on the second mark puts it after this date. Thus the first must be between 1784 and 1821 and the second between 1821 and 1837.

If you now look in your hallmark book

(Jacksons) at the London cycles of date letters for these periods you will see that an S appears only twice (1793 and 1813) between 1784 and 1821, and only once (1833) between 1821 and 1837, which must be its date. If you then compare the S of 1793 with that of 1813 you will see that the former has a small bar 'cut' through the middle of it, whereas the latter is plain which is what we have with this mark. It must therefore be 1813.

I hope this does not sound too complicated. Once you know the 'ground rules' I am sure you will find it quite easy.

Don't try to learn all the date letters. There are far too many, and to my mind it would be a complete waste of time.

Do remember the important dates when changes took place – they are very useful – and then always look the mark up in your hallmark book.

GOLD MARKS
Although gold is not the subject of this book, a few pointers may be useful.

Up until 1798 gold was marked in exactly the same way as silver (apart from a short period between 1697 and 1720 when the silver marks changed as a result of Britannia Standard).

The introduction of a new standard of 18 ct. (ct. = carat[1]) in addition to the existing 22ct. obviously required a new mark to enable the two standards to be distinguished from each other. For this a crown and the number 18 were used (sometimes combined, crown over 18 and sometimes as two separated punches) for 18ct. whilst 22ct. continued to be marked in the same way as silver until 1844.

During the mid-nineteenth century several new and lower standards came in – 9ct., 12ct. and 15ct., the 12ct. and 15ct. eventually being replaced by 14ct. in 1932.

Until 1975 all these lower standards were marked with a carat number together with a number indicating the gold content based on pure gold being 1. We have 15ct. = .625, 14ct. = .585, 12ct. = .5, and 9ct. = .375.

PLATINUM MARKS
These were introduced in 1975, an orb and cross within a pentagon being chosen as the mark. The standard is 950 parts per thousand.

PROVINCIAL MARKS
This is a fascinating area where, in most cases, the marks of a particular town or area are a complete study in themselves. (See *Jackson's Silver and Gold Marks.*) It is also an area of collecting where interesting discoveries may be found.

Broadly, provincial marking may be divided into three periods. These are:

Pre-1697
1697 - c.1701/2
1701/2 - present day

Before 1697 marks are found from numerous centres. Some of these such as York and Norwich had been officially appointed in 1423 to assay silver but most such as Exeter and King's Lynn had not.

Marking in these centres ranges from the use of a maker's mark only at its most basic through to centres such as York which had a similar system to London. An interesting characteristic is that when only one or two marks were in use these were often repeated to give the visual impression of a set of London hallmarks.

The period between 1697 and 1701/2 is of great academic interest since nowhere other than London was legally permitted to assay. This was due to a mistake made by Parliament in the bill introducing Britannia Standard. They forgot to include any provincial centres. The marks have the same characteristics of the pre-1697 period but most individual marks were changed.

The year 1701 saw the appointment of York, Exeter, Bristol, Chester and Norwich as centres where Assay Offices could be operated, to which Newcastle-upon-Tyne was added in 1702. All of these centres were to use marks

---

1. Carat. Measure of purity of gold. Pure gold is 24 carat, 18 carat = 75% gold content.

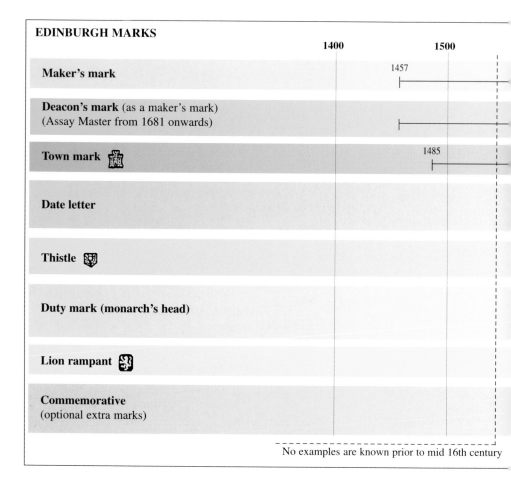

EDINBURGH MARKS

	1400	1500
Maker's mark		1457
Deacon's mark (as a maker's mark) (Assay Master from 1681 onwards)		
Town mark		1485
Date letter		
Thistle		
Duty mark (monarch's head)		
Lion rampant		
Commemorative (optional extra marks)		

No examples are known prior to mid 16th century

the character of which was the same as those used in London but to which was added a town mark.

These marks are often confusing, especially so because York in particular often omitted its town mark. The marks then look like a rather odd set of London marks. It is not unusual to find people suspecting that they are forgeries of London marks.

It is always a good idea to check where the maker was actually working. For example, just because a piece has an Exeter hallmark does not mean that it was made there. The goldsmith may well have been working in Plymouth but would have had to send it to the Assay Office in Exeter. The piece should therefore be more accurately described as Plymouth silver marked in Exeter. It makes it much more interesting.

Mention should be made of Birmingham and Sheffield. Assay Offices were established in both cities in 1773 and much of what is found today is from these centres. They are also the only provincial centres still assaying in England.

The choice of a crown for the mark of Sheffield (up to 1975 when it was replaced by a rose) and an anchor for Birmingham may appear rather odd. The explanation is simple. When in 1773 they were petitioning Parliament for the establishment of their Assay Offices their meeting place was The Crown and Anchor Tavern in Westminster!

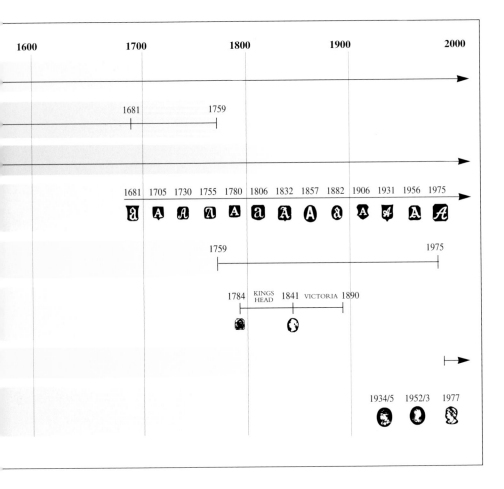

| 1600 | 1700 | 1800 | 1900 | 2000 |

1681   1759

1681 1705 1730 1755 1780 1806 1832 1857 1882 1906 1931 1956 1975

1759   1975

1784 KINGS HEAD 1841 VICTORIA 1890

1934/5 1952/3 1977

Scotland

Edinburgh

Scotland had developed and used its own system of marking until Edinburgh (by the mid-eighteenth century) and Glasgow (in the early nineteenth century) came into line with the English (London based) system.

The standards used before the early eighteenth century were also different (20ct. for gold and 91.66% minimum silver content for silver). These had come into effect as a result of an enactment of 1457 which also required pieces to have a maker's mark and a Deacon's mark (the Deacon was the chief office bearer of the craft in the town). Since the Deacon would also have been a working goldsmith he would, when in office, use his maker's mark for this purpose.

This would of course result in what would appear to be two makers' marks on a fully marked piece. (This is however academic since no piece of marked Scottish silver is known to survive before the mid-sixteenth century.)

In 1485 a further enactment added a town mark (castle). From that date until 1681 three marks were struck on a piece. As a rough, but by no means absolute guide the castle will usually be the central mark with the maker's mark to the left of it and the Deacon's to the right.

Dating is based on knowing the years of office of the various Deacons. This is however complicated by the fact that a man may have held office for more than one year with several

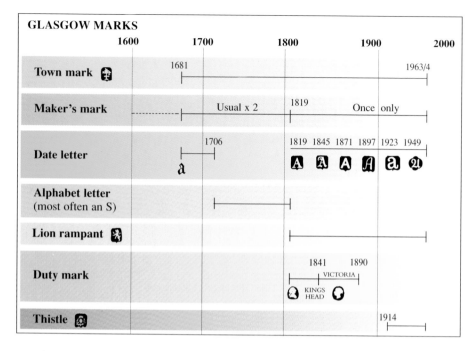

GLASGOW MARKS

	1600	1700	1800	1900	2000
Town mark		1681		1963/4	
Maker's mark		Usual x 2	1819 Once only		
Date letter		1706	1819 1845 1871 1897 1923 1949		
Alphabet letter (most often an S)					
Lion rampant					
Duty mark			1841 1890 VICTORIA / KINGS HEAD		
Thistle				1914	

years' gap between years of office. George Craufuird, for example, was Deacon in 1615-6-7 and again in 1621-2 and finally in 1633-4-5.

   1633/5 Edinburgh

Sometimes the maker's mark may help. The above example has the maker's mark of Thomas Kirkwood. He was not admitted into the Corporation until 1631 and therefore a piece struck with these marks would have to be from 1633-4-5.

From 1681 onwards Edinburgh marks become easier. Date letters were introduced, and the deacon's mark was replaced by the Assay Master's mark. The Assay Master, like the Deacon before him, used his own maker's mark so there still appear to be two makers' marks on a piece. In 1759 the Assay Master's mark was replaced by a thistle which in turn was replaced by a lion rampant in 1975. Duty marks, as in London, appear between 1784 and 1890. There was no provision for Britannia Standard marks in Edinburgh until 1908-9.

Edinburgh – Useful Key Dates

Pre-   Three marks. Castle, maker's
1681   mark and Deacon's mark (usually looks like a castle with a maker's mark on each side).
1681   Date letter added.
1759   Thistle mark used (Assay Master's mark – formerly Deacon's mark – ends).
1784   Duty mark added.
1890   Duty mark ends.
1975   Lion rampant replaces thistle mark.

Scottish Provincial

For those who love collecting interesting marks this is one of the best areas to concentrate on. There are two good reasons for this. First there are a large number of centres, some quite obscure, and secondly most of the pieces to be found are spoons (particularly tea), ladles etc. from the late eighteenth/early nineteenth century. They are affordable and it is an area of collecting where discoveries are still to be made.

Identification of centres is often very easy, many abbreviating their name, for example ABD for Aberdeen, BAF for Banff and INS for Inverness.

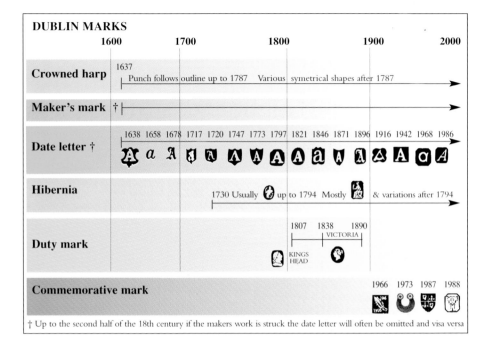

DUBLIN MARKS

	1600	1700	1800	1900	2000
Crowned harp	1637 — Punch follows outline up to 1787 Various symetrical shapes after 1787 →				
Maker's mark	† — →				
Date letter †	1638 1658 1678 1717 1720 1747 1773 1797 1821 1846 1871 1896 1916 1942 1968 1986				
Hibernia			1730 Usually up to 1794 Mostly & variations after 1794 →		
Duty mark			1807 1838 1890 — VICTORIA — KINGS HEAD		
Commemorative mark				1966 1973 1987 1988	

† Up to the second half of the 18th century if the makers work is struck the date letter will often be omitted and visa versa

The repeating of marks to give the visual impression of the four or five marks in use in Edinburgh is usual.

Be prepared that you may acquire the odd piece of colonial, particularly Indian (see page 24) silver by mistake. Many Scots provincial silversmiths emigrated to the colonies and quite naturally continued to mark their pieces in the same manner as they always had done back in Scotland.

Glasgow had an established Assay Office from 1819 until its close in 1964. Before this (apart from a cycle of date letters between 1681 and 1705) the marks are usually: town mark (tree with fish etc.), maker's mark, usually repeated twice, and a letter of the alphabet, usually an S, which is often mistakenly believed to be a date letter.

Glasgow – Useful Key Dates
Pre 1819 Provincial style mark.
1819   Town mark, lion rampant, date letter, duty mark and maker's mark.
1890   Duty mark ends.
1914   Thistle mark added.
1963/4   Assay Office closes.

Ireland

Dublin

By a Charter of 1637 silver and gold was to be marked with a crowned harp and a maker's mark. The following year a date letter was added.

For nearly one hundred years these remained the only marks until, to show the payment of duty, the Hibernia mark was added in 1730 (a very useful date to remember).

As a result of the Act of Union in 1807 the monarch's head was added. This replaced Hibernia (which became the Dublin mark) as the duty mark and was similar to that already in use (1784 onwards) in England and Scotland and continued as elsewhere until 1890.

Two important points to remember:
1. *Don't* confuse Hibernia with Britannia (Hibernia rests her arm on a harp – Britannia on an oval shield).
2. During the mid-eighteenth century it is usual to find incomplete marks. If a maker's mark is struck then the date letter will often

21

be omitted, and vice versa. Of the two it is more desirable to have a piece with a maker's mark and no date letter rather than date letter and no maker's mark.

Dublin – Useful Key Dates

1638-1730	Crowned harp, date letter, maker's mark.
1731	Hibernia added.
1807	Duty mark added.
1890	Duty mark ends.

Irish Provincial
You are most likely to find pieces from Cork; after that, and far more seldom, Limerick. Anything else is exceptionally rare.

The style of marking you are most likely to come across in Cork and Limerick is much the same – variations of the word STERLING stamped in full together with a maker's mark. The marks, particularly makers, are often repeated.

Distinguishing Cork from Limerick is best done by looking up the maker to see where he was working. Do remember that vast quantities of American silver are found stamped with the word STERLING.

FOREIGN/CONTINENTAL MARKING
All European countries and many others have at some stage marked silver in some way. The degree of control and the complexity of each system has varied greatly, each being a study on its own.

To say that it is a minefield is an understatement. For many countries there is little or no easily accessible and/or reliable published work.

Matters are also made no easier by the extensive forgery that has gone on, and still does, in many areas. We are very fortunate in Great Britain that our laws have been both so strict in themselves and so strictly enforced that little forgery is found here (see Chapter 15, page 166).

To give a useful guide I have selected below those countries whose marks you are most likely to encounter.

America
Since there was no guild system and no other form of control, each silversmith chose his own form of marking.

Makers' marks using initials only are found particularly in the seventeenth and eighteenth century. The use of the full surname was much favoured. Some makers were particularly helpful and stamped in addition the name of their town or city.

Some particularly early nineteenth century pieces may be marked COIN indicating that they were made out of melted silver coinage or that they were the same standard as the coinage and thus implying that they should be of good standard.

The vast majority of pieces encountered today will be stamped with the word STERLING together with the maker's name or initials. They will usually have been made within the last one hundred to one hundred and fifty years.

An example of a Paul Revere of Boston mark, c.1760.

Maker's and sterling mark of Joseph Rice of Baltimore, Maryland, c.1780. Bonhams

Austro-Hungarian
The system established for the Austro-Hungarian Empire was based on the earlier marks of Vienna. In Vienna, instead of using separate marks to indicate the city, date and standard these were, as they were gradually introduced, incorporated into the one punch. As long as the mark is clear dating after 1675 is easy since the year is given in full.

Vienna Prior to 1675		Town
Vienna 1675/1737		Town and date
Vienna 1737/1784		Town, date and standard (15 lot)
Vienna 1784/1806		Town, date and standard (13 lot)

Austro-Hungarian Marks

From 1806 onwards a letter at the top of the punch indicates the city

1806-1866 15 lot* 13 lot*

A. Vienna
B. Prague
C. Salzburg
D. Lvov
E. Cracow (1807-09)
E. Hall (1824-1866)
F. Brno
G. Linz
H. Graz
I. Klagenfurt
K. Ljubliana
L. Trieste

From 1867 onwards a head is used and the date is no longer given.

1867-1872

950/1000   900/1000   800/1000   750/1000

1872-1922. The letter indicates the city

950/1000   900/1000   800/1000   750/1000

A. Vienna
B. Linz
C. Prague
D. Brno
E. Cracow
F. Lvov
G. Graz
H. Hall up to 1872
H. Bregenz after 1872
K. Klagenfurt
L. Ljubliana
M. Trieste
N. Zadar 1866/7
P. Zeit
R. Kovice
T. Timsoara
U. Alba Lulia
V. Zagreb

* Lot:- Standard used extensively in Central and Eastern Europe.

16 = 100%
15 = 93.75% (equivalent to Sterling)
14 = 87.50%
13 = 81.25%
12 = 75%

Belgium

Before the establishment of the Kingdom of Belgium in 1831 marking is dependent on under whose control the area was.

Up to 1797 a town mark together with a year mark and a maker's mark was in use. Antwerp, for example, used a hand with a crown above.
Antwerp 1765

Town   Date   Maker

Between 1797 and 1831, the area changed hands

French   Netherlands
1797/1815   1815/1830

In 1831 a new system was established based on French marking

Purity   Guarantee of test

1869 saw the end of obligatory control. Purity marks were used up to 1942 – makers' marks were not however necessary.

1869-1942

900/1000}
                          small items
800/1000}

900/1000}
                          large items
800/1000}

23

British Colonial

Many silversmiths established themselves in various colonies producing work for the settlers and colonial officials.

Having produced their work it was expected by their customers that, since it was silver, it should therefore be 'hallmarked'. The silversmiths obliged and produced their own versions of the marks that they had known from wherever they had originated. This results in many colonial pieces bearing pseudo English or Scottish marks.

By far the largest area of production was India with many firms (often of Scottish origin) operating. Hamilton & Co. and Twentyman & Co., both of Calcutta, were the most important.

Other important centres were established in South Africa, Australia, Canada and New Zealand.

Interestingly, such was the output in Jamaica in the mid-eighteenth century that an Assay Office was established there. Others such as Barbados are to be found, but, production in these smaller centres was on a tiny scale.

Much silver was made in England and exported to the colonies. This can clearly be seen from the number of pieces of English manufacture found with colonial retailers' marks stamped in addition to the English marks supplied in cases with the name of the colonial retailer in the lid.

Marks

Australia

Canada

Jamaica

China Trade

A number of Chinese silversmiths developed businesses in Hong Kong, Canton and Shanghai, to supply the market for silver largely created by visiting European merchants as well as resident Europeans.

The earliest of these were in Canton at the turn of the eighteenth/nineteenth century. The end came in the 1920s. Most prolific was Wang Hing who operated in both Canton and Hong Kong from the 1870s to the 1920s.

Marks fall into three groups:

a. Chinese characters

b. Pseudo English (as with colonial)
c. Chinese characters plus maker's mark in often rather shaky roman characters

Denmark

Before 1685 a town mark and maker's mark were all the requirements necessary.

In 1685 a very precise system was introduced for Copenhagen. This required not only the town mark which now had the year in full below it but also a mark (a sign of the Zodiac) for the month as well as an assay master's mark and a maker's mark.

Hamilton & Co. (India)

Twentyman & Co. (India)

South Africa

Example

In 1893 new legislation required the official town mark with the year (now abbreviated), the assayer's mark, a number giving the purity of the silver in parts per thousand with the letter S and the maker's mark.

Town and date   maker   assay master

Since 1977 the town mark has no longer incorporated a date. Marking has been voluntary for some time with many silver-smiths using personal marks.

Example

France

The most ancient and at times complex of all systems. Essentially divided into Pre- and Post-Revolution.

Pre-Revolution – up to 1789/90
Large pieces of silver

Charge   Warden   Discharge   Maker
1775/81   1775   1775/81

Taking Paris as our example. the mark by which it is most easily recognised is a crowned, often very elaborate, letter A. This was the charge mark of the 'Fermier' who was responsible for collecting the duty or tax on silver and was stamped on the silver in the raw after the maker's mark and before the Warden's mark.

The Warden's mark, which was put on after the silver had passed Assay, may be regarded as the 'date letter', it is a crowned letter of the alphabet.

The piece was then made by the goldsmith from the already tested and marked silver. This is why, incidentally, genuine French marks of this Pre-Revolution period are frequently badly distorted.

On completion of the piece the goldsmith then had to take it back to the Fermier and pay the tax due. Having done this, or having discharged his obligation, a final mark – the discharge mark – was stamped by the Fermier. Discharge marks are very small.

French Provincial

Different crowned letters of the alphabet were generally used by the Fermier to indicate the various *départements,* for example

B: Rouen   M: Toulouse   R: Orléans

Large pieces of silver

Toulouse 1789   Warden   Discharge   Maker
Charge

Problems

Since crowned letters of the alphabet were used for both the Fermiers' marks and the Wardens' marks (date letters), confusion can very quickly set in.

Also, there are many oddities, and exceptions, together with a completely different set of marks for gold and small silver wares. In addition always remember that there are numerous fakes.

If you develop a headache and at times give up in frustration when dealing with French marks I will not be in the least bit surprised. Good luck!

Post Revolution

Everything had to change. A Law of 1791 abolished all the Guilds, but it was of course soon realised that some form of proper control was necessary. The goldsmiths as a result were made an exception and reinstated for a short period (until 1797).

From 1798 onwards a new system of marks was introduced. These indicate first the standard (1st 950/1000 silver and 2nd 800/1000 silver). The first of these was a cockerel (used up to 1819 and then replaced by a head). The shape of the punch together with the position of the cockerel and the number 1 or 2 indicates whether it is Paris or provincial.

The next is a tax mark. At first (up to 1838) this is a head with a number or device incorporated to indicate the Assay Office.

Since 1838 the head of Minerva has been used as a standard mark. A tiny boar's head (Paris) or crab (provincial) mark is found on many pieces. This is a restricted warranty mark and indicates when found that the piece is approximately of the standard.

French makers' marks from 1797 onwards are easy to recognise. They are always in a lozenge-shaped punch and will usually have a symbol in addition to the makers' initials.

An unusual feature of French marks after 1818 is the anvil or reverse mark, introduced to counteract forgery. The 'anvil' on which the piece was held to strike a mark and which is normally smooth was itself engraved so that it also marked the piece. Thus, if you examine behind, for example, a standard mark you should see the anvil mark (insects were very popular).

Some French silver will be found with both pre and post-1791 marks. This indicates that the piece was still in stock at the time of the Revolution and had to be re-tested and marked to meet the new requirements before it could be sold.

Silver 1809/1819

Paris
1st Standard Silver

Assay
Medium size piece

Head of Minerva used, with variations,
1838 to present day.

Germany

Each principality had its own marking until 1888, usually the town mark and a maker's mark.

The two most important centres were Augsburg, with its famous pineapple mark (of which there are numerous variants) and Nürnberg which conveniently used an N as its mark.

From 1888 onwards marks for Germany, as opposed to the principalities, are found. The crescent enclosing a crown was first used at this time and is usually accompanied by the number 800 (denoting 800 parts for 1000 silver). Vast quantities were produced using this standard during the late nineteenth and first half of the twentieth century. It is one of the marks that you are most likely to encounter.

   Augsburg

   Nürnberg

 . 800   Germany 1888 onwards

Pitfalls
Large number of nineteenth century forgeries of early 'German' silver. There was apparently little control at this time and many took advantage of this.

Italy

No unified system existed until recently and each area/town had its own marks. It was Napoleon who in 1810 introduced a system based on that of France.

In 1873 a new system came into effect with standards of 800, 900 and 950. This in turn was changed in 1935 with 800 and 925 standards only being used.

Attitudes to the use of these marks has been rather liberal.

1810-1872

large item	small item
800/1000	950/1000

large item	small item
950/1000	800/1000

1873-1935

950/1000	900/1000	800/1000

1935 onwards

925/1000	800/1000

The Netherlands

A good system of marking has existed for many centuries with Amsterdam and S'Hertogenbosch known to have been using date letters since 1503.

Up to 1663 a town mark, maker's mark and (with the more important centres) date letter should be found.

Leiden 1655

From 1663 until 1807 a crowned lion rampant was used by most important centres.

The Hague, 1757

The period between 1807 and 1812 sees the use of French style marks.

From 1813 to 1953 the lion rampant has been used with the number 1 to denote 1st Standard (833/1000).

1814-1953

934/1000	833/1000

Since 1953 roman numerals have been used with I for 1st Standard (925/1000) and II for 2nd Standard (now 835/1000).

1954 onwards

925/1000	835/1000

All centres have used the same date letters from 1813 onwards.

Pitfalls

There are a great many forgeries. Vast quantities of pseudo early silver was produced in the late nineteenth/early twentieth centuries. There are so many fakes that a book of fake hallmarks has been published in the Netherlands

The use of the lion passant for 2nd Standard has confused many. Always remember that the Netherlands lion is facing right, the English lion (with only extremely rare exceptions) faces to the left. Look also for the number 2 under the lion; this is only ever found on Netherlands silver.

Portugal

Up to the introduction of the state system in 1881 a standard of 958/1000 was in force with towns having their own marks. In addition to this, a maker's mark would also be found.

Oporto Lisbon
18th century   18th century

A provisional state system was introduced in 1881 followed quickly in 1886 with an obligatory one. Under this standards of 916 and 833 parts per 1000 came into effect.

1886-1938 Lisbon (with possible variation of 5/1000)

large work

916/1000   833/1000

small work

916/1000   833/1000

Lisbon (possible variations 2/1000)

small work

916/1000   833/1000

large work

916/1000   833/1000

New legislation in 1938 brought about the present system.

Modern Post 1938 Lisbon

large work

916/1000   833/1000

small work

916/1000   833/1000

Russia

The vast majority of pieces encountered will be from either Moscow or St. Petersburg. Most will date from the late eighteenth through to the early twentieth century.

The town mark of Moscow is easy for any Englishman to remember – St. George and the dragon (post 1741). That of St. Petersburg is crossed anchors and a sceptre.

Dating, so long as the marks are clear, could not be easier. The date is given in full either under the town mark (as part of it) or under the assay master's initials.

The number 84 when found denotes the standard and is the equivalent of 873.5/1000 silver.

In 1899 a new system of marking came into effect. This combines the standard and town mark, and comprises (from left to right) in an oval punch (1) a number denoting the standard, (2) a girl's head facing left, (3) the initials of the assay master from which the town can be deduced. The order changed in 1908 to (1) a Greek letter to denote the assay district, (2) a girl's head facing right, (3) a number denoting the standard.

Not surprisingly, this marking ended in 1817. In 1927 a similar head was introduced, now however with a hammer. In turn this was replaced in 1958 by a star enclosing a hammer and sickle.

Makers' marks are naturally Cyrillic initials, sometimes with the name in full. Look out for a Romanov eagle combined with the maker's mark. This indicates that the maker held an Imperial warrant – only the most important got these.

Marks

Moscow

St. Petersburg

1899-1908

1908-1917

1927-1958

Maker's mark Carl Fabergé (Note the eagle above)

Spain and Spanish Colonial
Early marks (sixteenth and seventeenth century), comprise a town and makers mark. The town mark is usually its name either in full or abbreviated.

Barcelona   Cordoba

In Mexico assayers', quality and tax marks were used e.g.

Between 1881 and 1934 marking was entirely voluntary. Since 1934 a quality mark (915 or .750) and a makers mark have been required.

915/1000   750/1000

Letters are used to indicate the official testing laboratories, e.g. M for Madrid, B for Barcelona and SE for Seville

Sweden
Early marks (prior to 1689) comprise a town mark and a maker's mark. In 1689 date letters were introduced in Stockholm. The system was expanded in 1758 to include the rest of the country.

In 1860 letters of the alphabet were used to denote the different assay offices.

The most distinct mark is the state control mark of three crowns introduced in 1752 and still in use today.

Swedish year marks use a combination of letters and numbers. As an example, A is 1759, A2 is 1783 and A3 is 1807.

Making Silver

In order to understand antique silver it is very important to have some idea of how it was made.

As we have seen, silver is one of the most wonderful materials to work with, being one of the most malleable and ductile of all materials known to man.

Most work is carried out when the metal is at room temperature. When heat is required the temperatures are easily accessible (silver melts at 960.5°C).

The most important tool in silversmithing is the hammer. Go into any silversmith's workshop and you will find a wide range of shapes and sizes of these. The silversmith is above all else a hammerman.

MAKING SILVER

To understand the basic principles and in turn the 'jargon' that you may come across when a piece is described, it is probably best to look at the different ways in which a piece may be made. Taking as our example a pear-shaped coffee pot, there are three principal ways in which the body of this may have been made:

1. Raising, 2. Seaming and 3. Spinning

1. Raising

The full description of this is 'hand raising from the flat'. This is the best way to make a piece, but also the one that requires the most work. As a result it is, of course, the most expensive.

The silversmith starts with a disc of silver.

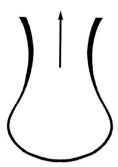

Cross section showing the thickening of the body which results from the raising process.

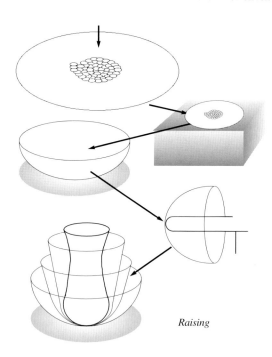

Raising

Today he would buy this from his bullion supplier. At earlier periods he would have made this himself from an 'ingot' which he would have cast (see below).

The disc is first hammered in concentric circles against a stake (the silversmith's equivalent of an anvil), starting in the centre and working out. Known as forging, this squeezes the silver between the hammer head and the stake and stretches it. By not hammering the edge this remains the same diameter. Having, however, stretched the silver in the middle, it has to move somewhere and so forms a 'saucer shape'.

Having achieved this 'saucer shape' the silversmith switches to the raising technique. Here the silver is held against the stake and struck with a raising hammer just above the point of contact with the stake. This pushes the silver down on to the stake. It does not stretch it, as it does with forging, but 'gathers' the silver up, making it thicker. With a 'deep raising', such as a coffee pot, the top when finished may be two or three times thicker than the base. This gives great strength where it is needed.

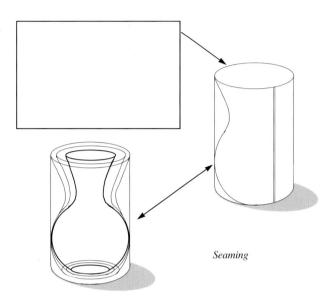

Seaming

As the silver is hammered it gets harder. This is known as 'work hardening'. When this happens the silversmith heats it until it is red hot and then plunges it into water (known as quenching). This softens the silver and makes it workable again. This whole process is known as annealing.

Each time annealing is carried out the silver never becomes quite as soft as it was the time before. As a result, with a coffee pot body, where this may have to be done about thirty times during the course of raising, the silver is much harder and tougher when the body is completed than it was initially.

With a hand raised piece if you feel the thickness between your finger and thumb you will often notice that at the very top it is much thicker. This is achieved by the silversmith hammering straight down on to this edge after each successive course of raising. It is always a very good indication of quality if this thickening, known as caulking, is present. Do not be fooled by wires that have been soldered on afterwards.

2. Seaming

This technique was and still is used on a very large scale. Its advantage is that it reduces significantly the time needed to make a piece.

An oblong sheet of silver cut to the required size is wrapped round to form a cylinder and the seam (the join where the two sides meet) is soldered (see below).

Having made a cylinder the silversmith, if necessary as in this case, turns to the raising technique to achieve the final shape.

A disc is then soldered into the base (usually the foot is soldered on at the same time) and the body of the pot is complete.

A useful point to remember when examining a piece is that as the seam may be seen (solder is slightly 'yellower' than silver) the silversmith will usually position the handle so as to cover the seam, thus helping to conceal it.

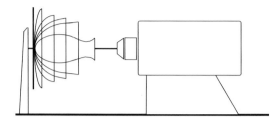

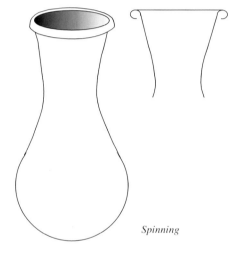

Spinning

3. Spinning

A technique which developed with the Industrial Revolution (late eighteenth/early nineteenth century) and which has been used particularly in mass-production.

The shape of the object to be made is first formed out of wood or steel. This is known as the chuck. If it is a shape where the top is narrower than any point below it, it has to be made like a Chinese puzzle so that it can be extracted piece by piece after the silver has been spun around it.

A thin disc of silver is then tightly clamped against the chuck and the motor is turned on. As the chuck and silver spin together the silver is forced against the chuck. The tool to do this looks rather like an enormous screwdriver.

The top edge is then either turned back on itself or it may have a wire soldered on to it. This makes the top rigid. A disadvantage of turning the top edge back on itself is that damage to such an edge is usually extremely difficult (if not impossible) to repair.

Having looked at the three principal ways in which the body of a piece may be made, the following points should help you to tell when examining a piece which technique has been used.

Taking a pear-shaped coffee pot as our example:

Hand Raised
No Seam
'Hammer' marks on inside, usually smooth on the outside.
Usually a very good weight (feels nice and chunky when picked up).
Solid top edge (often caulked).

Seamed
A vertical seam usually at the back (the handle is normally positioned over this).

Soldering. Solder is silver to which brass has been added to reduce its melting point. It is made to a variety of melting points. 'Hard solder' is a very high temperature solder (just under the melting point of silver). Easy flow solder at the other extreme has a much lower melting point.

There is a good reason for these different melting point solders. You may have to solder two or three times during the making of a piece. By starting with a high melting point solder and then moving on to successively lower melting point solders you will not melt your previous solderings, undoing what you have already done.

Looking into the pot you should see the disc soldered in to form the base.

'Hammer' marks on inside, usually smooth on the outside.

Usually, but not always, a good weight.

Solid top edge (usually an applied wire).

Spun

No Seam

Very smooth inside, often with fine horizontal spinning lines showing. Usually smooth outside. *However* some manufacturers hammered over the body of spun pieces to give the impression that they were hand made.

Usually very light weight.

A turned over (hollow) top edge always indicates a spun piece. A solid wire may be found instead.

Other Techniques

Casting

Casting is essentially a technique where the metal is melted and poured into a mould of the desired shape. When the metal has cooled and solidified the mould is broken away leaving the casting.

Castings are usually thicker than sheet metal

Casting. Detail of cast stem of centrepiece..
Sotheby's

parts and consequently heavier. The inside or underside of a casting is usually left quite rough.

Entire objects (e.g. candlesticks) may be made using this technique alone, or parts of objects (e.g. spouts, handle sockets, feet etc.).

Stamping

A thin sheet of silver is placed between two steel dies. These have the desired shape cut into the lower one and the exact opposite 'raised' from the surface of the upper one. By dropping (which is carefully controlled) or using some form of mechanical pressure on the top die, the silver sheet is forced between the two, taking on the shape of the die.

This was and still is used a great deal in mass-production for the making of such pieces as bon-bon dishes, photograph frames, dressing table sets and loaded (filled) candlesticks.

If the piece is not filled, such as a bon-bon dish, it will be very light and flimsy. (Often with wear and tear it will be full of holes and will most likely have the odd split.)

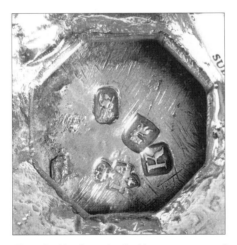

The underside of a casting (in this case an octagonal foot) left in its rough state.

Stamping. An example of poor quality. Notice that the decoration does not match up at the seam.

Private collection

Above left: Filigree.   Sotheby's

Above. Chasing.   Sotheby's

Stamping may also be found on pieces of the highest quality. Decoration such as King's pattern on spoons and forks was achieved by die stamping.

Filigree
Fine wires are twisted into decorative patterns and soldered together building up the piece. Although this produces a very delicate object, some surprisingly large pieces (e.g. caskets, inkstands, candlesticks) have been made using this technique.

Small pieces are however the norm: bon-bon dishes, card cases, caddy spoons, little boxes etc.

It is very delicate and highly susceptible to damage. Any damage is difficult to repair satisfactorily so do examine pieces very carefully.

Chasing. Notice how from the inside you see the reverse of what is on the outside.   Sotheby's

Flat chasing.   Sotheby's

DECORATING SILVER

Repoussé, Chasing and Embossing

These three terms tend to be used very loosely. In all cases the silversmith, having formed the desired object, uses a variety of punches to decorate it.

To support the metal during this process either a sandbag is used or the piece is filled with or set on pitch. This gives the necessary support and control.

Repoussé. The object is hit from the back producing bumps on the surface.

Chasing. It is hit from the front, indenting the surface.

Embossing. Often misused today to describe repoussé. It is, however, a combination of the above two. Most such decoration starts by being hit from the back to give the basic shape. The detail is then punched in from the front.

Flat Chasing

The decoration is punched from the front only leaving the basic surface as 'flat' as when the chaser started. Flat chasing is often mistaken

Flat chasing. The ghost impression found with flat chasing.   Sotheby's

for engraving, but it is very easy to distinguish the two. Flat chasing will have a 'ghost' impression on the back. Engraving will not.

Engraving.   Sotheby's

Bright-cut engraving.   Private collection

Engraving
Lines are cut into the surface. This actually removes silver. The lines are cut out, *not* scored into the surface (as happens with a scratch). Apart from decoration this technique is the one most commonly used for armorials, crests, initials and inscriptions.

Bright-cut Engraving
Developed during the last quarter of the eighteenth century, facets are carved into the surface. These reflect the light at different angles giving a 'sparkle' to the decoration, hence bright-cut.

Engine Turning
A mechanical form of engraving first used in the second half of the eighteenth century in France and became popular in England in the early nineteenth century. It was mainly used on snuff boxes, vinaigrettes and card cases.

Engine turning.   Bonhams

Gilding, silver gilt and parcel gilt

The description silver gilt is given to a piece made out of silver completely covered with gold.

Parcel gilt refers to an object made out of silver and only partially covered with gold. (The word parcel is a corruption of partially).

Methods of gilding

Fire/Mercurial Gilding

Powdered gold is mixed with mercury forming an amalgam. This 'paste' is then painted on to the object wherever gilding is required. The object is then heated (originally placed in the fire, hence the name). As the temperature increases the mercury is driven off, leaving the gold fused to the surface.

It is the finest form of gilding known, but there is a snag. The mercury vapour driven off is extremely poisonous and would eventually kill the people doing it. As a result of this problem the process was made illegal after the introduction of Electro Gilding.

Electro Gilding

Developed in the early nineteenth century, gold is deposited using an electrolytic process (see Electroplating page 163.)

Applied Work

Cut-Card.

Used mostly in the late seventeenth/ early eighteenth century. A decorative shape is cut from a sheet or card of silver and soldered on where required.

Gilding.   Sotheby's

Parcel gilding.   Sotheby's

Above: Cut card.   Sotheby's

Above right: Cast and applied.   Sotheby's

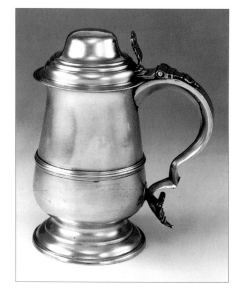

Wire (moulded girdle).   Sotheby's

Cast and Applied

Decorative sections are cast separately and soldered on to the piece.

Wire and Mouldings

Either plain wire or wire which has been decorated (e.g. beading) soldered on to a piece. Tankards and two-handled cups frequently have a wire (referred to as a girdle) applied around the centre or near the centre of the body.

Note – Possible Confusion

With all three of the above techniques when looking inside you should see little (sometimes a slight ripple) or no sign of the decoration which appears on the outside. If you do see the reverse of the external decoration then you should look to either Embossing/chasing or Stamping as the technique. (Girdles may be spun.)

Piercing

Here the technique is to cut holes through the silver either for a practical purpose such as the top of a sugar caster or for purely decorative effect.

There are three ways in which this may be done – chiselling, cutting with a piercing saw, or mechanical piercing. (The last two developed in the latter part of the eighteenth century.)

Other techniques

Burnishing
Polishing by means of a very hard, and very smooth, steel or agate burnisher. Many different sizes and shapes of burnishers are used, each suiting different surface configurations. These are literally rubbed (burnished) over the surface using considerable force. Stale beer was normally used to lubricate the surface whilst this was done. It was traditionally women's work. Sadly it is rarely done today, machine polishing having largely replaced it.

Planishing
This is part of the finishing process. When a silversmith has finished raising, the surface will be covered by quite pronounced hammer marks left by the raising hammer. To get a good, smooth surface the piece is then planished.

A much smaller and lighter hammer which has a highly polished face is used for this. The piece is held firmly against the stake and hit so that the silver is 'squeezed' between the hammer head and the stake. It has to be hit just hard enough to move the silver from the high to the low points but not so hard as to stretch the silver.

The process is repeated, each time with lighter hammer blows until the desired surface is attained. A skilled man can virtually polish a piece using this process.

With the majority of pieces the surface was smoothed further (using various stones) and then burnished (see above) and finally polished. It did however become a feature of Arts and Crafts pieces (by The Guild of Handicraft) to leave a planish finish to their pieces. This was then copied and exaggerated to varying degrees by others (e.g. Omar Ramsden). Taken to its extreme you find 'Spot Hammered' pieces (see below).

Etching
Used mostly in the nineteenth century. The surface was covered with wax which was then cut through, the pattern or scene etc. showing as exposed silver. It was then put in acid which ate into the exposed areas. The wax would later be removed leaving the etched decoration. Variation could be achieved by exposing some areas to the acid for longer periods than others.

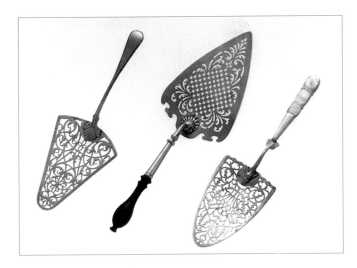

Piercing. Phillips

39

Spot Hammering

An exaggerated form of planishing where the surface is hammered with a domed face hammer leaving pronounced concave depressions.

Enamel (Cloisonné, Champlevé, plique-à-jour)

Enamel is really a glaze fused to the surface. It may be opaque or translucent. There are three techniques which you will come across. To understand these it is best to take them in historic order.

Cloisonné

Used in England up to the twelfth/thirteenth century when it was largely replaced by Champlevé. It was revived in the nineteenth century. Many pieces are from Russia where the technique has been used extensively. Wires are soldered to the surface forming small compartments or cloisters (hence the name). Enamel is placed in these and fired, fusing the enamel into the compartment. The wires do two things – separate different colours and give the 'skeleton' of the design.

Spot hammering. Private collection

Cloisonné. Christie's

Champlevé (also known as Limoges)

Most of the enamel work you will come across will be of this type.

Developed in Limoges, the surface is carved to provide the separate compartments. By the fourteenth century this had been refined so that by carving to various depths and using a translucent enamel 'shading' could be achieved (the deeper the carving, the darker the colour). It also became possible with improved technique to do away with the divisions that had been required between different colours.

Plique-à-jour

This is very easy to identify. Just hold it up to the light and if it looks like stained glass with the light shining through then it should be plique-à-jour.

Rarely found on English work, it was popular in Scandinavia and Russia, particularly for small spoons and ladles.

Champlevé. Bonhams

Plique-à-jour. Bonhams

41

Niello.   Bonhams

Pricking.   Sotheby's

Niello

A very ancient technique, it was used to decorate Roman silver. Most examples you come across will be Russian and most of these will be nineteenth or early twentieth century.

Niello is a black compound made by fusing silver, lead, sulphur and copper together and then powdering it. The surface to be decorated is carved where the niello is to be and filled with the compound. After firing it is 'polished' back to the original surface leaving the carved areas filled with niello. The contrast of the

black niello against the white silver is very effective. Since niello is a metallic alloy it is less susceptible to damage than enamel.

Matting

A surface made up of lots of tiny 'pimples'. It was often used as a background giving greater visual depth to decoration. In the mid-seventeenth century alternate horizontal plain and matted bands were a popular form of decoration.

Pricking

Decoration or initials built up from a series of 'pin pricks'. It was popular up to the end of the seventeenth century and continued to be used for initials after that.

Punching

A crude form of flat chasing (see page 35) using a simple punch to build the decoration. This was usually done at speed – cheap and cheerful! Very popular in the seventeenth century.

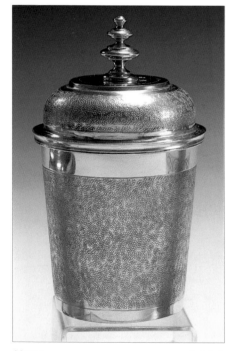

Matting.   Sotheby's   *Punching.*   Sotheby's

CHAPTER 5

Makers

The maker's mark which is struck on a piece will in most cases not necessarily be the mark of the person who actually made the piece.

There are a number of reasons for this. Most pieces are the product of a workshop where a number of different craftsmen will use their particular skills at various stages in the making. One may do the hand raising, another the casting, yet another the assembly, and finally another the polishing. Each will have contributed to the piece but the mark finally struck will be that of the master who owns and runs the workshop. (He/she will probably have not physically worked on the piece at all, indeed may not even be a qualified silversmith, but the piece will today be referred to as having been by him/her.) Thus a piece described as being by Paul de Lamerie or Paul Storr is most of the time from their workshops rather than by them personally.

Even this may not be the case. It is known, for example, that one maker would sometimes pass work through the assay office for another who did not have a registered mark. Paul de Lamerie was on several occasions in trouble with the Goldsmiths' Company for passing the work of 'strangers' through the assay office with his own maker's mark struck on the piece.

It was also common practice for work to be brought in already marked from a specialist (for example, a spoon or candlestick maker) and for the retailer to overstrike the existing maker's mark with his own. A good example of this is the mark of George Grey which is commonly struck over that of various members of the Bateman family.

Most recently manufacturers have simply produced pieces which have then received the mark of the firm which is going to retail the piece. This is why today it is no longer referred to as a maker's mark but as a sponsor's mark.

There are of course exceptions to this where it is known that a silversmith was working on his own, but they are rare exceptions.

Charles Robert Ashbee
(The Guild of Handicraft 1888-1908)

It was Ashbee who put the ideas of William Morris into effect for the making of silver. This was a revolution against mass-production. Every piece had to be made using traditional workshop methods (hand raising, etc.) using a small group of craftsmen who worked together to create the object, each using his own particular skill.

Final planishing marks were left in to show that the piece had been hand made. The use of wirework (particularly for handles) and the setting of cabochon stones are both characteristic of Ashbee's designs.

The Batemans
Hester Bateman (fl. 1760?-1790, London)

The most famous (and arguably the worst) woman silversmith in England. A brilliant businesswoman, she built up what had been a component manufacturers to the trade into the largest manufacturing silversmiths in London at the end of the eighteenth century. She supplied the new retail outlets of the period with stereotyped pieces. Although these often give a pretty visual impression they rarely stand up to close scrutiny either in design or execution. Her spoons and forks, which are mostly of average quality for the period, together with some very pretty wine labels, are probably the best pieces.

The other Batemans

On Hester's retirement in 1790 her sons, Peter and Jonathan, took over the running of the company. Jonathan died just four months after this and his widow Ann took his place in the partnership.

In 1800 Wm. (Hester's grandson) became a partner with his mother and uncle and continued with his uncle after Ann's retirement in 1805. When Peter retired in 1815 the firm continued with Wm. Bateman registering a mark on his own account.

The quality of Bateman work steadily improves as it gets later. Indeed, Wm. Bateman was a very fine goldsmith who produced some of the top pieces of the late Regency/early Victorian period.

Bateman collectors always pay a premium for pieces by Peter and Jonathan. This is on the basis of rarity, the mark having been used for such a short period. It should, however, be remembered that twelve weeks' production of the Bateman factory would provide more silver than many individual makers would make in a lifetime! The Peter/Jonathan mark is rare in terms of Bateman marks but is not a rare mark when a broader view is taken.

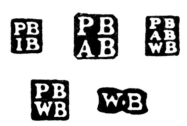

Matthew Boulton
(Silver and Old Sheffield plate, fl. mid-1760s-1809, Birmingham)
Matthew Boulton Plate Company (1809-1840)

Having built the Soho Works on Handsworth Heath, Birmingham, between 1759 and 1766, Matthew Boulton, with his partner Fothergill, started to produce the finest Old Sheffield plate ever made, together with some of the best neo-classical silver.

Before the opening of the Birmingham Assay Office in 1773 (through Boulton's efforts), the silver was sent to Chester for marking.

His finest work is from the period up to the late 1770s when James Wyatt appears to have been responsible for many of the designs.

Having found that there were problems with supplying the aristocracy, at whom he had first targeted his work, little silver was produced in the 1780s and early 1790s. By the late 1790s, however, through taking a new direction and supplying the rising middle class market, production increased again.

After Boulton's death in 1809 the impetus appears to have gone and the business steadily declined until it was finally sold in 1848.

Paul Crespin (1694-1770, London)

Without question one of the great masters, the equal of Paul de Lamerie with whom he clearly had a close working relationship. (Important commissions were sometimes shared between them.) The scale of his production is much smaller than that of de Lamerie which is probably why he is less well known today.

Crespin produced some of the masterpieces of rococo silver. Perhaps the most extraordinary piece of eighteenth century silver was made by him for the King of Portugal – a bath weighing about 6,030oz. (830kg). Sadly the fate of this remarkable piece is not known.

Dr. Christopher Dresser (1834-1904)

Included here not as a goldsmith, which he was not, but because of the importance of the silver/electroplate designs he produced in the late 1870s/early 1880s.

These are startling, even today. They were not only the first true 'industrial designs' but also the introduction of functionalism into design.

The majority of his designs were for Hukin and Heath for whom he became design consultant. Others were for Elkingtons and for Dixons – amongst his most extraordinary and sometimes most eccentric being the teapots he designed for the latter.

Elkingtons
(Mid-19th-mid-20th century, Birmingham)

This extraordinary firm, which made its fortune initially through holding the patent for electroplating, is a dominant factor in the nineteenth century.

Its wealth enabled it to employ craftsmen from as far afield as Japan. It also meant it could employ top designers such as Leonard Morel-Ladeuil and commission designs from Dr. Christopher Dresser. From just these two names it will be realised that an enormous diversity of style will be found – always with a very high standard of craftsmanship.

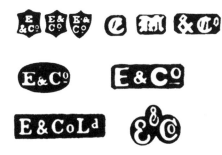

Andrew Fogelberg
(fl. c.1770-1793, London)

Andrew Fogelberg's Swedish origins and training bring a slightly different approach to the neo-classical silver of the period. Always of top quality, a distinctive feature of much of his work is the use of silver castings of classic cameos applied to the pieces. He worked from 1780 in partnership with Stephen Gilbert (who had been trained by Edward Wakelin) until his retirement in 1793 when his workshops were acquired by Paul Storr (q.v.).

There is evidence to suggest that on his retirement he returned to Sweden.

The Foxes – Charles, Charles Thomas and George (19th century, London)

A fascinating family of goldsmiths whose flowering was very much with the partnership of Charles Thomas Fox and George Fox in 1841

They used a wide range of design sources both geographically and historically. They did not, however, go in for the eclecticism which typified so much of the period but managed to produce their own distinctive form (particularly of the rococo).

The Foxes present a great area for collecting. Not only is there a very wide range in size, type and style of objects but prices are, for most pieces, still modest.

Pierre Harache I and II
(fl. c.1682-1700 I?, c.1698-1705 II, London)

Pierre Harache I was the first of the Huguenots to be admitted to the Freedom of the Goldsmiths' Company at the end of the seventeenth century. One of the greatest goldsmiths ever to work in England, he was succeeded in 1698 by his son who continued to supply the top end of the market with silver of the same superb quality.

Their important works include the Burghley toilet service of 1695 and the ewer and sideboard dish of 1697 (formerly at Chatsworth) made by the father. From the son we have the magnificent Marlborough ewers and dishes together with a wine cistern and fountain of 1701.

If new research is correct, the father was dead by 1690 and the pieces attributed to him between 1690 and 1698 should be assigned to his widow.

Thomas Heming
(fl. 1745-early 1790s, London)

Having been apprenticed to Peter Archambo, Heming was one of the few to produce fine rococo work during its usually rather decadent dying phase in the late 1750s/early 1760s. He was appointed Principal Goldsmith to the King in 1760 and went on to produce some of the great pieces of English neo-classical silver.

He lost his royal appointment in 1782 as a result of a 'witch hunt' on expenditure within Government departments (is there anything new?)

Charles Frederick Kandler
(fl. 1727-1778, London)

With his very long working life Kandler unusually produced work which covers the entire stylistic range of the eighteenth century from formal baroque through rococo (of which he was one of the masters) to neo-classicism.

Of German origin, there have been several (unsuccessful) attempts to link him with the

famous Kandler of Meissen porcelain.

His greatest known surviving work has to be the wine cistern of 1734 in the Winter Palace at St. Petersburg. Designed and commissioned by Henry Jerningham at just short of 8,000 Troy oz. (about a quarter of a ton or 250kg!) and holding some sixty gallons (273 litres), it is the largest single piece of eighteenth century English silver known.

Paul de Lamerie (fl. 1713-1752, London)

One of the greatest Huguenot goldsmiths whose family had fled from France. Apprenticed in 1703 to Pierre Platel (q.v.), his talent was quickly realised and he was appointed a Subordinate Goldsmith to the King in 1716, only three years after completing his apprenticeship in 1713.

Having produced superbly designed and executed work up to the early 1730s, he then became and remained the great leader of rococo silver in England until his death in 1752. His workshops must have been the largest in London during this period since more work survives by him than anyone else at the time.

Anthony Nelme (fl. c.1660-1722, London)

Arguably the finest of the English goldsmiths working at the time. His establishment must have been of some size judging from not only the number but also the scale of his surviving pieces.

His work is of the same quality as his contemporary Huguenots.

His business can be traced down to the present day – Barnards are his direct descendants. Amongst his more important works are the candlesticks of 1694 made for St. George's Chapel, Windsor, and the pilgrim bottles of 1715 at Chatsworth.

Anthony's son, Francis, was another great goldsmith, albeit on a smaller scale.

Pierre Platel (fl. 1699-1719, London)
The equal of few and second to none, Platel not only produced some of the greatest surviving goldsmiths' work but also was the master of Paul de Lamerie (q.v.). His most important known surviving work is the small gold ewer and dish made in 1701 for the Duke of Devonshire.

Rundell, Bridge & Rundell
(Late 18th early 19th century, London)
An extraordinary firm developed by Philip Rundell in the late eighteenth century which went on to dominate the Regency period, having been appointed goldsmiths to the King in 1797.

Rundell was the, not very pleasant, driving force behind the business. His partner John Bridge was very much the courtier who would deal with the important clients. They were so opposite in temperament that they were known as oil and vinegar (Bridge the former, Rundell the latter).

What, apart from Rundell's driving force, appears to have made the business so successful was his choice of both great craftsmen (Digby Scott and Benjamin Smith, Benjamin and James Smith and Paul Storr (q.v.), all produced for the firm) and great designers (Flaxman, Baily, Stothard, Thead and Pugin all designed for Rundells). In the case of the latter it was actually John Bridge who discovered Pugin (working on some Dürer drawings in the British Museum), recognised his talent and gave him his first commission.

Rundells supplied most of the great banqueting services and other major silver of this period. It was with the decline of Rundells after Philip's retirement in the early 1820s that Garrards (q.v. under Wickes) were able to take over as Royal Goldsmiths in 1830.

John Scofield (Schofield)
(fl. last quarter 18th century, London)
One of the few important goldsmiths of the late eighteenth century, he excelled in two particular areas – the making of candlesticks/candelabra and the mounting of glass. Other pieces by him (his range was extensive), although of top quality, rarely exhibited the same brilliance.

Do not assume that all his candlesticks are absolutely top flight. It is clear that he supplied a wide price range and that at the bottom end he appears to have been buying in mass-produced candlesticks from Sheffield and retailing these under his name.

Nicholas Sprimont
(fl. c.1742-c.1747, London)
One of the great masters of the rococo, his work, which is extremely rare, is often of a highly sculptural form. He turned in the late

'40s from silver to porcelain production with the founding of the Chelsea porcelain factory. There may have been an early association with Paul Crespin (q.v.), who was a near neighbour.

Much of his surviving work is in the Royal Collection.

Paul Storr (Storr & Mortimer, Mortimer & Hunt, Hunt & Roskell, London)

Born in 1771 and apprenticed to Wm Rock, Storr began his working career in partnership with Wm. Frisbee in 1792. This partnership was shortlived and Storr registered his first mark on his own account in 1793. His pieces in the early 1790s, although exhibiting the high quality of workmanship for which he is justifiably famous, showed no artistic flair. They are simply top quality standard late first period neo-classical pieces.

It is with such important commissions as the gold Portland font of 1797 that really exciting artistic developments began. From here on his growing association with Rundell, Bridge & Rundell (q.v.), which culminated in a partnership in 1807, is of great importance. The reason was simple: Rundells commissioned designs from leading designers of the period, thus the technical skills of Storr combined with the artistic talent of the designers resulted in some of the most important pieces to be made at the height of the Regency.

In 1820 Storr severed his links with Rundell, Bridge & Rundell. After this, although the technical brilliance remains the artistic merit is often lacking. Storr was clearly a great technician capable of executing brilliantly the designs of others, but apparently lacking artistic talent himself.

In 1882 he entered into a disastrous partnership with John Mortimer, resulting in the loss of most of the fortune he had built up during his Rundell, Bridge & Rundell years. The firm was saved by John Samuel Hunt who provided capital and became a partner.

When Storr retired in 1838 the firm continued as Mortimer & Hunt until 1843 when it became Hunt & Roskell and Hunt & Roskell Ltd. in 1897. They were acquired by Benson in 1889. Aspreys have recently resurrected the name, Hunt & Roskell Ltd., it having previously ceased trading in 1965.

Throughout the entire history of the firm the standards established by Storr were maintained. Storr himself died in 1844 and was buried in Tooting.

Anne Tanqueray (fl. c.1726-d.1733, London)

To my mind the greatest of the women goldsmiths. The daughter of the great David Willaume, she had married David Tanqueray, an apprentice of her father's, in 1717, and had continued the business (very much an offshoot of her father's) after David's death in c.1725.

In both 1729 and 1732 she is recorded as a Subordinate Goldsmith to the King.

Subsequent generations of the Tanqueray/ Willaumes moved into the church, and from there into gin!

George Wickes/Wakelins/Garrards (fl.1722-today, London)

George Wickes founded a great goldsmithing dynasty. Having registered his first mark in 1722 he went on to establish himself by the 1730s as the leading English (as opposed to Huguenot) goldsmith of his day. In 1735 he was appointed Goldsmith to Frederick, Prince of Wales. By that time he was also supplying many members of the aristocracy.

Of particular importance are the pieces made by him to the design of William Kent, the most famous of which is the Pelham gold cup of 1736.

Edward Wakelin, having joined the firm in 1747 when he entered his first mark which very closely resembles Wickes', steadily took over the silversmithing side of the business with Wickes becoming a sleeping partner.

Wakelin in turn went into partnership after 1758, first with Parker (the firm becoming Parker & Wakelin) and then in 1776 with his son John and William Taylor (Wakelin & Taylor). This became Wakelin & Garrard in 1792 and Robert Garrard I in 1802, from which the present day Garrards is directly descended.

The firm's status as Royal Goldsmiths is fascinating. Having been Goldsmith to Frederick, Prince of Wales, and supplied pieces to his son, the future King George III, they had fully expected to be made Royal Goldsmiths in 1760. However, Heming (q.v.) was appointed instead and it was not until the decline of Rundells (q.v.) that they finally received the appointment in 1830 which they hold to this day.

There is from the point of view of the silver scholar/historian/enthusiast a marvellous piece of 'icing on the cake'. In 1952 nearly all the ledgers of the firm back to 1735 were discovered (the eighteenth century ones are now in the Victoria and Albert Museum). These have taught us not only about the eighteenth century goldsmithing trade but have

also solved many problem over the use of certain objects, e.g. the fact that cake baskets were really bread baskets or that the argyle was really for gravy.

If you have an eighteenth century piece by a member of the firm (post 1735) and you can identify the original owner, then it should be possible to find the piece in the accounts.

David Willaume
(fl. in England c.1686-c.1728, London)

One of the great Huguenots. His origins were in Metz where it is most likely that he trained. On arrival in England in the mid-1680s he set about establishing what became one of the most important goldsmithing establishments of the period.

His business in Pall Mall became the hub of a fascinating 'family' group which includes Lewis Mettayer (brother-in-law), David Tanqueray (son-in-law), Anne Tanqueray (daughter) and David Willaume Jun. (son). From the evidence of surviving pieces it is clear that work was farmed out around the family.

He was clearly an important member of the Huguenot community, being witness to many marriages (including that of Marie Mettayer to the great engraver Simon Gribelin) and becoming godfather to many children.

Many major works survive. These include sideboard dishes and ewers for the Dukes of Abercorn, Buccleuch, etc., wine coolers for the Duke of Devonshire and a wine cistern and fountain for the Duke of Brunswick.

CHAPTER 6

Spoons and Flatware

Spoons are the only examples of early silver that it is possible to collect. Examples can be acquired from the Roman period through to the present day. The only really difficult area is the Dark Ages, but then they are pretty difficult for everything.

Not only is there a tremendous range of period but there is also a great range of size, type and price. This means of course that anyone to whom spoons appeal can find examples to collect in a price range in which they feel comfortable.

From the Medieval period through to the mid-seventeenth century they were the most personal of all pieces of silver. At the time of your baptism you would be presented with a spoon. What you got depended on the wealth and status of your family. If you were a peasant – wood or horn. You then moved up through pewter to brass. Once you reached the ranks of

1 (Far left). Roman (ligula), 4th century AD. About 7in. (18cm) long.
Phillips

2 (Left). Dark Ages, probably 5th/6th century. The Roman example (1) will look much the same from this angle.
Phillips

3 (Right). Diamond point, late 14th century. The fact that it is marked adds significantly to its value.
Sotheby's

the well-to-do merchants, yeoman farmers and so on up through society then you would be presented with a silver spoon. As a result being 'Born with a silver spoon in your mouth' really did have a great social significance.

The spoon you received at your baptism would be the one you used for the rest of your life. At banquets you were expected to take your own spoon and knife. None would normally be provided.

If you were working your way up through society, then upgrading your spoon was important – a silver spoon normally being your first, and, for many, only piece of silver. Some even 'cheated' and had brass spoons silvered to make it look as though they were higher up the social scale than they actually were.

Conversely when, for whatever reason, you were disposing of your silver, your spoon would be the last thing to go. It is, in this context, hardly surprising that so many early spoons have survived.

The evolution of the spoon is fascinating, starting with the Roman silver *ligula* (No. 1). This is a direct translation into metal from a much earlier organic form – essentially a mussel shell with wooden handle attached. It is interesting that *cochleare,* one of the Latin words for a spoon, was also the word for a shell.

In the context of this organic form the 'rat-tail' found on the back of the bowls of Roman and many later spoons is easy to understand. Originally it would have been an extension of the handle, giving the necessary support to the shell bowl.

The Roman form evolved steadily through to such elaborate forms as the Coronation spoon. Then, during the first half of the thirteenth century, spoons developed rapidly into the Early English form which continues up to the mid-seventeenth century.

Characteristically an Early English Spoon will be between about 6in. and 7in. (15 to 18cm) long, have a fig-shaped bowl, a stem of hexagonal cross section, and (with the exception of slip tops and stump tops) a finial on the end of the stem.

This finial, which may take many forms, is

4 (Left). Slip top, London 1506. Notice the reverse taper of the stem. Christie's New York

5 (Right). Apostle spoon, London 1609 (St. Thomas). Notice the almost parallel stem by this period. Sotheby's

referred to as a knop and it is by the type of finial or knop present that these spoons are known, e.g. Acorn Knop, Seal Top and Lion Sejants.

Most famous of all are the Apostle spoons which date from the late fifteenth century through to the mid-seventeenth century (No. 5). These should not be confused with the many 'Apostle' coffee and teaspoons which are found in very large numbers from the turn of the nineteenth/twentieth century.

Although Apostle spoons were made in sets, most were sold as individual spoons. Complete sets, of which a few survive, comprised thirteen spoons, twelve apostles and a master spoon. Each apostle is identified by a symbol – St Peter a key, St Andrew a saltire, St John a cup etc. The Master is usually Christ giving a blessing with his right hand and holding an orb and cross in

hallmarked the Assay Office would deliberately strike the date letter at the top of the stem away from the other marks. This made it easy to catch anyone trying to add a finial after marking.

Both the above are important to remember since enterprising individuals have in the past been known to cut the tops off the more common seal tops in the hope of making more money by selling them as slip tops.

Puritan spoons are the transition between

6 (Left). Puritan, mid-17th century.   Phillips

7 (Right). Trefid, c.1660-1700.   Sotheby's

his left. Mary may be found as an alternative to Christ as the Master. Such full figures of Mary are, however, exceptionally rare.

Early English spoons without finials are found from the fourteenth century through to the mid-seventeenth century. Two types are found – slip tops and stump tops. The slip top gets its name from the heraldic word 'slipt' meaning 'cut off'. In both cases the stem tapers in the reverse direction. Spoons with finials taper from the bowl to the finial. Slip and stump tops taper towards the bowl.

Marking is also different and quite distinctive on slip/stump tops. Spoons with finials will, taking London as an example, be marked with the leopard's head in the bowl and all other marks on the back of the stem near the bowl. If, however, a spoon had no finial when

8 (Left). Dog nose, London 1708.   Christie's New York

9 (Right). Rat-rail, Edinburgh 1721. In this case a basting spoon, 14¼in. (35.7cm) long.   Sotheby's

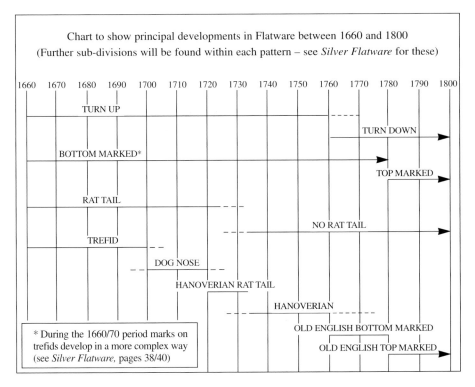

Chart to show principal developments in Flatware between 1660 and 1800

(Further sub-divisions will be found within each pattern – see *Silver Flatware* for these)

* During the 1660/70 period marks on trefids develop in a more complex way (see *Silver Flatware*, pages 38/40)

Early English and modern spoons. Made in the mid-seventeenth century, their name results from their plain form which is essentially that of a slip top but with a much broader stem (No. 6).

Radical developments occurred as a direct result of the Restoration of the Monarchy in 1660. Charles II, having been in exile on the Continent, had naturally acquired Continental eating habits which he was certainly not going to alter because of his return. These were adopted by members of his Court and so started to spread down through society.

This change was given greater impetus at the end of the century as a result of William and Mary coming to the throne and, in their train, the arrival of the many thousands of Huguenot (French Protestant) refugees.

Most important of the changes were the acceptance of the fork and the development of the flatware service. Forks had been known and used earlier. It is however clear that they

had been regarded as rather foppish, and that no real man would use one!

During the late seventeenth century examples with two, three, four or even five prongs were produced. Three prongs became the norm, followed a long way behind by two, and remained so until c.1760 (four or five prongs are very rare).

The concept of providing your guests with knives, forks and spoons was revolutionary. It is no wonder that they referred to them as table knives, forks and spoons, since they were of course the first to be produced specifically for setting on the table. As others were added they were given names appropriate to their use – dessert spoons, teaspoons, coffee spoons etc.

This was the start of flatware as it is known today or spoonware as it was referred to earlier this century and before. Silver spoons and forks should never be referred to as cutlery. Cutlery refers to the knives.

10. Hanoverian, mid-18th century (back view).
Christie's New York

11. Old English (top marked), late 18th century and on (back view). Christie's New York

Important changes occur as flatware develops. The dates at which these happen are well worth remembering since they will help to narrow down the period of production of any piece which is original to period and not a reproduction.

Flatware may first be divided into two major groups based on whether the spoons turn up or down at their end.

Turn up flatware dates from between 1660 and 1760. Spoons and forks at the time were set in the French manner, i.e. open bowl facing the table – this is why original engravings of crests/initials etc. will be on the back of the stem.

In about 1760 fashion changed – spoons were now set with the open bowl up. As a result the end of the stem now turned down. Crests etc. were now engraved on the front.

There is some overlap between turn up and turn down, mostly in the 1760s. Forks throughout continued to turn up (for comfort). They changed, however, from three to four prongs at this time.

During the twentieth century many patterns have been produced with straight ends to their stems.

Another broad, and very useful division is between top and bottom marking.

By the end of the seventeenth century marks were grouped at the bottom of the stem. There they remained until about 1780 when they were moved to the top of the stem.

From the nineteenth century onwards many of the decorative patterns were marked nearer to the middle of the stem.

Within the broad category of turn up flatware further divisions may be made.

As a result of the French influence, rat-tails reappear on the backs of the bowls of spoons in the 1660s and continue until about 1730. Thus any turn up spoon with a rat-tail should date from between 1660 and 1730, without it it should be between 1730 and 1760/70.

The rat-tail group itself may be further broken down by pattern:– trefid c.1660-1700, dog nose c.1700-1720 and Hanoverian with rat-tail c.1720-1730.

The first of the turn down spoon patterns was the Old English. This, with its decorative variants such as Old English Bead (edge) and Old English Thread (edge), dominated flatware production until the very beginning of the nineteenth century.

The important switch during the early 1800s was to the Fiddle pattern (No. 12) which had dominated French flatware in the eighteenth century but did not find much favour in Britain until the Regency.

From here on the emphasis is on increasing elaboration with Fiddle Thread, and Fiddle Thread and Shell, leading on to Hour Glass, Kings', Queen's etc. (see *Silver Flatware*).

Most of the patterns from the Old English onwards have, with varying degrees of popularity, continued through to the present day. In addition the earlier patterns began to be revived during the latter part of the nineteenth century so that today a very wide range is available.

Flatware terminology

Service. A set of twelve of each table and dessert spoons and forks together often with teaspoons. (Knives, since they are usually modern, are regarded separately.)

Half Service. Literally six of each as above.

Turn up/Turn down. See text above

Bottom marked/Top marked. See text above.

Double struck. With die-struck decorative patterns such as King's, this refers to the decoration being on both the front and the back.

Single struck. Die-struck decoration on the front with a plain back (mostly produced in Scotland).

Half. e.g. Half King's or Half Queen's. Only the top half of the stem is decorated. Most usually this will also be single struck. Hence single struck Half King's (the vast majority will be Scottish).

Straight. A service which is all of the same date and by the same maker.

Harlequin. An assembled service comprising a variety of dates and makers.

Bastard. A variant from a standard pattern or an odd size.

Heel. The area at the back of the bowl at its junction with the stem.

Drop. Basically the small 'heel' left over as the last vestige of the rat-tail. There are several variations (see *Silver Flatware*, page 84).

Fancy Back. The back of the bowl of mid-eighteenth century spoons decorated with a shell, scrollwork or a combination of both.

Picture Back. As for fancy back but with a 'picture' such as a crown, double headed eagle, ship, dolphin etc.

Building a service

This can be both fun and rewarding if tackled in the right way.

1. Choose a pattern that you like.
2. Make sure that it was made in all the sizes you require. (Some patterns were only ever produced for dessert services).
3. Check that it is in the price range that you feel comfortable with.
4. Try to acquire the dessert forks first and then match other pieces to these.

For further information see *Silver Flatware*.

12 *(Left). Fiddle pattern (with thread edge), early 19th century and on.* Christie's New York

13. *(Right) King's pattern, 19th century and on.* Sotheby's

CHAPTER 7

Lighting

1. Early/mid-17th century. Note the very wide drip pan at the base of the stem. This is always a distinctive feature of early examples. (This example is a modern copy.).
Christie's New York

CANDLESTICKS

There are essentially three ways in which the vast majority of candlesticks you come across will be made: cast, loaded and sheet silver.

The easiest way to tell which you have is to turn one over and look at its base. If it is cast or sheet silver you should see only silver. If loaded then you will be confronted most usually with a baize covered base, a piece of wood, or a metal plate (if any of these are missing then the pitch or plaster filling may well be showing).

Sheet silver examples are easy to distinguish from cast ones. The former will be smooth inside and of even thickness (size for size they will also always be much lighter). The latter will be quite rough underneath with only the centre smooth where it has been turned on a lathe.

As a very good guide (exceptions, leaving aside pre-late seventeenth century examples, are rare), the best are cast, then sheet silver and last the loaded examples.

Possible confusion may arise where a cast example has sometimes been loaded or where a loaded example has had its filling removed.

2. Charles II. This type often formed part of a dressing table set. Notice the 'drip pan' at the base of the stem – still there but much less pronounced.
Sotheby's

3. Late 17th/early 18th century. The most common of the 17th century forms and last of the sheet metal construction until the second half of the 18th century. Notice the last vestiges of the drip pan at the base of the stem. Sotheby's

The latter is very easy to tell since any such examples will feel light and flimsy. The reason, after all, for the filling is to give support to the thin sheet silver from which it will have been either stamped or spun. Sheet silver examples which have not been loaded will have been made from a sufficiently thick gauge of silver that they do not require the additional support.

The technique used to make a candlestick will give a very good indication of date.

Up to the end of the seventeenth century it would be quite exceptional to find anything other than sheet silver.

From the late seventeenth century through to

4. Late 17th century/very early 18th century. First of the cast examples. The lion marks on the top baluster add greatly to the value. Sotheby's

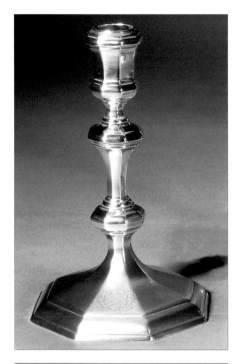

5. (Above left) Early 18th century. Highly desirable cast octagonal. Hexagonal examples may also be found. Sotheby's

6. (Above) Canted square, first quarter 18th century, cast. This particular form appears to have been favoured for some of the heaviest examples of this period. The illustrated example by David Willaume II, London 1729, weight in at 54oz. – 1679.56g (pair). Sotheby's

7. (Left) Shaped square, second quarter 18th century, cast. A very popular form produced in many variations. This example happens to be by Paul de Lamerie (London 1732). Sotheby's

the third quarter of the eighteenth century the vast majority were cast with a few sheet silver examples occasionally cropping up.

From about 1770 onwards loaded candlesticks rapidly took over with sheet silver examples occasionally being found together with some cast examples which continued to

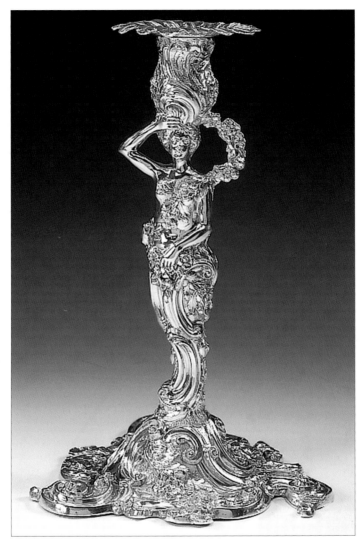

8. Rococo, mid-18th century, cast. Very fine rococo. The original of this design appears to have been by Paul de Lamerie. These are always taller than the normal shaped square examples.　　　　Sotheby's

be made for the top end of the market.

As a very broad guide size can during the eighteenth century give an indication of date (outside the eighteenth century size is too variable).

c.1700-c.1740	About 6in. (15cm)
c.1740-c.1755	7-8in. (18-20cm)
c.1755-c.1765	9-10in. (23-25cm)
c.1765-early 1800s	10-11in. (25-28cm)

9. Shaped square shell corner, mid-18th century, cast. A development from No. 7, it was also very popular and has many variations. Sotheby's

10. Hexagonal shell corners, mid-18th century, cast (unless made in Old Sheffield plate where they were amongst the first loaded sheet metal examples of the second half of the 18th century). These are normally taller than the square version (No. 9). Sotheby's

11. Square base baluster stem, mid-18th century, cast. One of the most desirable designs. (Also made in Old Sheffield plate. Sotheby's

12. Stepped square base, baluster stem, third quarter 18th century, cast. As with No. 11, a particularly sought after design. (Also made in Old Sheffield plate.) Sotheby's

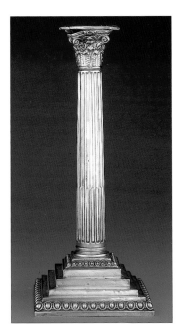

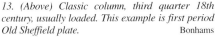

13. (Above) Classic column, third quarter 18th century, usually loaded. This example is first period Old Sheffield plate. Bonhams

14. (Above right) Neo-classic, 1770s. The design is attributed to Wyatt. They were made in Matthew Boulton's Soho Works. One of the finest candlestick designs ever. Christie's New York

15. (Right) Neo-classic, 1780s. Die stamped, loaded. Mix and match design. Very easy to find but not easy to find in good condition. Sotheby's

There will of course be exceptions to this but this guide should work for the vast majority of candlesticks produced during this period.

Points to look for
Candlesticks of all types are very prone to damage between the base and the stem. Always examine this point carefully for splits and/or repairs. (It is not unknown for candlesticks to be completely broken in two at this point.)

Be particularly wary of forgeries of cast examples (see Chapter 15, page 168).

Loaded candlesticks are especially vulnerable

16. (Far left) 'Neo-classic', c.1795/1805. Loaded. Very plain simple form, either oval or circular. Bonhams

17. (Left) Regency. Large, heavy and superb quality would sum up this top of the market example by Paul Storr. The majority of lesser examples are loaded (and a great deal less expensive). Sotheby's

to bruises which are very expensive to have taken out since the entire stick has to be dismantled. They are also (because the silver is usually quite thin) susceptible to wear. Always examine the high points and any sharp angles very carefully for signs of the pitch filling showing through. Again restoration will be expensive and in this case probably not worth while.

18. Telescopic – library candlesticks. Most examples are Old Sheffield plate and date from the very late 18th/early 19th century. Sotheby's

CANDELABRA

All candelabra are rare before the mid-eighteenth century. Their popularity increased rapidly in the second half of the century and the majority will date from the last quarter of the eighteenth century onwards.

As a rough rule of thumb the more lights (candles) an example has the later it will be with three lights being the most popular from the very end of the eighteenth century onwards. Five light candelabra are usually from c.1800 onwards.

The flexibility afforded by most candelabra is not often realised. Many pairs of three light candelabra, for example, will convert to a single four or five light (very useful for a round table), or a pair of two light.

Pitfalls

Branches are vulnerable to damage. Always pick them over very carefully for splits and old repairs. Recent marriages of sticks with branches are not a problem if they are a good match, you are told about it, and the marriage is reflected in the price.

It is not unknown for the central capitals of

2. Mid-18th century, cast two-light by Edward Wakelin. Christie's New York

1. Mid-18th century rococo, cast two-light by Paul de Lamerie. In this case the branches and sticks, although of a similar period and harmonising reasonably well, were not made together. Christie's New York

3. Neo-classic, late 18th century, loaded two-light. By this date they may be interchangeable two-three-light. Christie's New York

4. c.1800, cast two/three-light. The flame finial is detachable for conversion.   Christie's New York

5. Regency cast three-light (Paul Storr, 1814). Increasingly massive examples by this period. Gilding is common.   Christie's New York

6. 19th century cast three-light. Made by Garrards at the end of the 19th century to harmonise with a late Regency example by Paul Storr.   Sotheby's

7. Art nouveau c.1900, loaded. In this case American (New York). By the end of the 19th century quite small (these are only 10¾in. – 27.3cm – high) candelabra became increasingly popular.   Sotheby's

three-light branches to be swapped with the capitals of the candlesticks to make a marriage more convincing!

Any three light example before the very end of the eighteenth century should be treated with great caution. Most started life as two light and were converted to three light in the nineteenth century.

TAPERSTICKS

Examples may be found from the late seventeenth century onwards. Two principal types are found – the candlestick and the chamberstick form. In both cases the taperstick is a smaller scale version.

Their principal function was to melt sealing wax. It is therefore hardly surprising that inkstands were frequently made with them as a central fitting. (Many of the chamberstick form have a 'ring' underneath to fit on top of one of the pots.) Other uses were for burning aromatic tapers at the tea table (useful in the eighteenth century when few people washed) and for providing a flame to light churchwarden pipes.

Although the majority mirror the designs of contemporary candlesticks and chambersticks, some are distinct taperstick designs. The mid-eighteenth century harlequin is a good example, as are the chambersticks of vine leaf form found in the 1830s.

Not surprisingly, production declined rapidly in the 1840s with the use of envelopes after the introduction of the penny post. Reproductions of early eighteenth century examples have been produced since.

1. (Above left) Tapersticks from the Queen Anne to early George II period (starting with the earliest at the top left). Christie's New York

2. (Left) Inkstand with central taperstick. Sotheby's

3. (Above) Harlequin (mid-18th century). Sotheby's

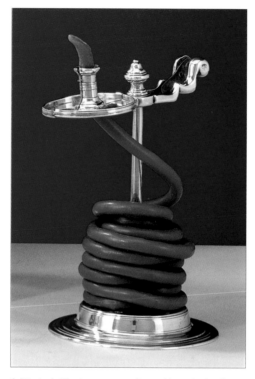

1. Waxjack. The less common form with vertical coil.
Christie's New York

WAX JACKS AND BOUGIE BOXES

These held a coil of wax which provided a small flame for the melting of sealing wax. Most found today are of eighteenth or early nineteenth century date.

The most usual form holds the coil horizontally in a frame. A less common form holds the coil vertically with the end held in a sprung scissor-like grip.

Bougie boxes are for the same purpose but hold the coil in a cylindrical box. In most cases these have a folding handle and swivelling cover for the aperture in the lid. It is reasonable, therefore, to suggest that these were a travelling version of the waxjack. The name derives from the French word for a candle.

2. Bougie box, late 18th century.   Private collection

CHAPTER 8

Tea and Coffee

COFFEE AND CHOCOLATE POTS JUGS AND COFFEE BIGGINS

During the late seventeenth/early eighteenth century both coffee and chocolate were popular drinks. The pots made for them are usually of identical form with the exception of the lid. The important distinguishing factor is that chocolate pots have a second 'lid' on top of the main lid. This was to allow a molinet or

'swizzle-stick' to be inserted in order to stir the chocolate before pouring. It is this and only this that distinguishes the two.

Since most swizzle-sticks had 'blades' at the bottom the lid was made with a detachable pin. This would be attached with a chain to the body of the pot to stop it being lost.

Many chocolate pots were converted to coffee pots from the mid-eighteenth century

1. Turn of the 17th/18th century. A rare early side handle form with spout ending with a bird's head. This shape should not be confused with the later 'tuck-in' base form (No. 6). Christie's New York

2. Tapering cylindrical side handle, Queen Anne. In this case a chocolate pot (notice the chain by the top handle socket). Bonhams

3. Octagonal, George I with handle in line. One of the most sought after shapes. Sotheby's

4. Tapering cylindrical side handle (second quarter 18th century). Squatter than No. 2 and with a flatter lid. This type is usually by Paul de Lamerie or one of the other Huguenots. Sotheby's

5. Chocolate pot, second quarter 18th century, with second lid removed. This example dates from 1741, unusually late for both the design and a chocolate pot. The explanation is that it was made in Exeter. Sotheby's

6. Tuck-in base, second quarter 18th century. This example has a replacement, silver, handle. The original would have been fruitwood. Sotheby's

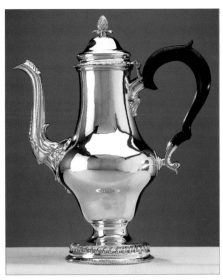

7. Pear-shaped, third quarter 18th century. A very popular shape. When chased, as this one is, be careful that the decoration is original. Sotheby's

8. Pear-shaped with drop bottom, 1770s if English. In this case American (Delaware c.1775).
Christie's New York

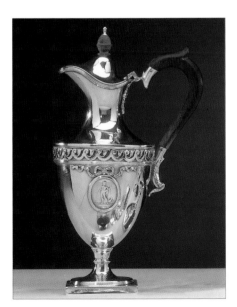

9. Neo-classic, 1770s and 1780s (in this case a jug).
Christie's New York

onwards by having their second lid soldered up. A quick look inside will usually indicate if this has been done (restoration is normally reasonably straightforward).

Few chocolate pots were made after the 1720s.

To work well a vessel for coffee should be tall and have either a spout set no lower than the middle, or a lip at the top. This is so that any dregs will settle at the bottom and not be poured out with the coffee. A pot with a low set spout will only be suitable for either instant coffee or those who have a taste for sludgy coffee.

It is worth noting that jugs are usually significantly cheaper than pots. At the same time they are far more useful. Unlike pots, which few people would use for anything other than coffee or chocolate, a whole variety of drinks may be served from a jug.

The majority of pots found up to the late 1720s will be of tapered cylindrical or, less frequently, octagonal form. These will have the handle either in line or at a right angle (side handle) to the spout. The popular misconception

10. Very late 18th/early 19th century. Made as part of a tea/coffee service to match the teapot. Spouts are sheet silver. If oval it will be 1790s; if oblong early 19th century, particular if, as with this example, it is on ball feet.　　　　　　　　Sotheby's

is that a side handle indicates a chocolate pot. This is not the case (see above).

By the 1730s the bottom starts to curve in (tuck-in base). This continues to develop in conjunction with a waisting of the upper body. The result is the very popular mid-eighteenth century pear shape, the last development of which is the pear shape with drop bottom found particularly in the 1760s.

As with teapots this steady evolution came to a fairly abrupt end with the introduction of neo-classicism. The simple pear shape, however, continued to be reasonably popular, particularly for jugs, until about 1790, and was produced at the same time as the classic vase-shaped pots.

Increasingly ivory was used for handles at this time, followed in the nineteenth century by the use of silver with ivory insulators.

During the late eighteenth/early nineteenth century coffee pots started to be made as part

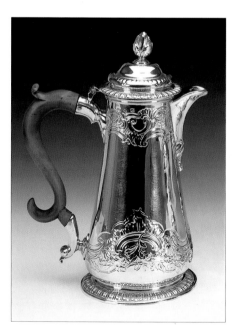

11. Mid-18th century jug. Same form as tuck-in base coffee pots of the period but much more difficult to find.　　　　　　　　Sotheby's

12. Mid-18th century jug. The most common shape, but with unusual 'ripple' decoration (explained by the fact that it is by Paul de Lamerie).　　Sotheby's

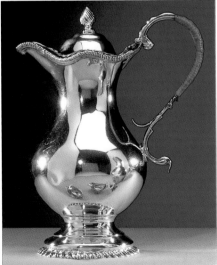

13. (Above left) Neo-classic, 1770/'80s. The less common classic vase. Notice the square pedestal which will normally put it into this date band.
Christie's New York

14. (Left) Third quarter 18th century. A more unusual example, the lip being part of the body and the top edge shaped. Notice the higher foot by this date. Christie's New York

15. (Above) Neo-classic, 1770s. Notice the plain area in the serpent handle where the wickerwork is missing (this is not a problem as replacement is quite easy). If the serpent were complete it would imply a claret jug. Bonhams

of matching tea/coffee services. Most usually these were based on the oval, through to the oblong bulbous form of teapot (see Tea/Coffee Services, page 88).

The design of this type of coffee pot was arrived at by increasing the depth of body of the teapot form and putting it on a pedestal foot. The result is not always happy, either from an aesthetic or a practical point of view, the practical problem being that the spouts are frequently placed too low (see above).

Coffee biggins are most popular during this same period. The name derives from their inventor – George Biggin. Characteristically they are of cylindrical or a slightly bulbous barrel shape. They have a lip with a strainer and are supported on a heater stand (many have now lost their stands). It is probable that they were originally intended for travelling or as a part of an officer's campaign equipment (No. 18).

Some rather fine Regency jugs of classic form were produced (in particular by Paul Storr). Many of these were originally supplied with heater stands (No. 17). More often than not they would originally have been part of a large tea/coffee service.

By the mid-nineteenth century a host of designs, often based on earlier forms, were in production with variations of the pear shape being most popular. Silver handles fitted with ivory insulators were standard by this time.

16. Neo-classic, 1770s. A superb example on heater stand designed by Wyatt. Asprey

17. (Above left) Regency, first quarter 19th century. Although on a heater stand, this design is described as a coffee jug, not a biggin, which is of essentially cylindrical form. This particular design is usually, as in this case, by Paul Storr. Sotheby's

18. (Above) Coffee biggin, first quarter 19th century. Complete and of standard design. Many have now lost their heater stands. Sotheby's

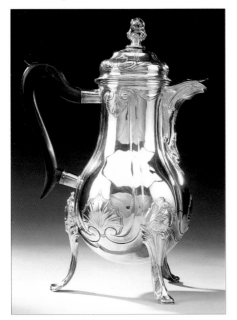

19. (Left) French mid-18th century form. Characteristically with pear-shaped body on three feet and often with a side handle. Found particularly in those countries most directly influenced by France. (This example is Belgian.) Christie's New York

1. Pear-shaped, first quarter 18th century. May also be found with side handle. This example is Irish.
Bonhams

2. Octagonal pear-shaped, late first quarter 18th century. Highly sought after shape. An original heater stand is always a plus. Sotheby's

TEAPOTS

Tea was first mentioned in England in the early seventeenth century. At first it was advertised as medicinal and was supposed to cure everything from gout to various social diseases.

Exactly how and in what it was first made is the subject of much debate and conjecture. The earliest known example dates from 1670 and is only recognised as a teapot by virtue of the contemporary engraving on it referring to 'This pot for tea'. Were it not for this it would be regarded today as a coffee pot.

By the late seventeenth century recognisable, if at times rather eccentric, teapots are found. Most are egg shaped. It was still an experimental period; lids have both finials and thumb pieces. Handles were often made of silver covered with either leather or wicker work. The end of the spout would at this time be provided with a hinged flap or a detachable 'stopper' (usually on a chain).

By the early eighteenth century pear-shaped and bullet-shaped pots became popular (outside museums these are the earliest examples

3. Shaped 'octagonal pear shape' (Germanic), second quarter 18th century. Found in Germany and countries influenced by German design. (This example is Belgian.) Sotheby's

that you are likely to come across). In both cases these may be either circular (most common) or octagonal – any other shape would be rare. Handles are now made of fruitwood (apple or pear).

Hinged flaps on the ends of the spout die out

4. Pear shape (Dutch), second quarter 18th century. Distinctly Dutch version of the pear shape with chased decoration. The genuine ones are usually quite light. Phillips

5. Bullet, mostly first half 18th century. May also be found octagonal. Any other shape is rare (but both six and seven sided versions are known). Sotheby's

6. Scots bullet, c.1725/c.1770. The spherical body, silver handle and high foot are all distinctly Scots features. Until the second half of the 18th century most have straight spouts. Sotheby's

7. Inverted pear, third quarter 18th century. Very short-lived form. This example is American (New York c.1765). Christie's New York

by the 1720s, as does the pear shape leaving the bullet in its circular form to dominate the second quarter of the eighteenth century.

A very short-lived form was produced in the 1750/60 period, during the last phase of the rococo – the inverted pear shape.

All teapots up to this point were, with only rare exceptions, of a small size. This was a direct result of the high price of tea.

With the reign of George III two important changes occur. First, with a reduction in the price of tea there is a marked increase in size.

8. Dutch 'inverted pear', third quarter 18th century. Distinctly Dutch form (usually quite tight if genuine). Phillips

9. Drum, 1770s. Very short-lived form. If it has a very thin curved spout look inside – it may be an argyle (a type of gravy pot with liner for water). Sotheby's

10. Oval straight-sided, 1780s. Standard form, usually quite light. The concave band between the sides and lid usually indicates that it is by Hester Bateman. Sotheby's

11. Shaped oval, 1780s/'90s. This example American (Boston, dated 1801). Christie's New York

Secondly, with the introduction of classicism there is a radical change in design, first in the 1760/70 period to the drum shape (which is fairly scarce), then from the '70s onwards to the straight-sided oval. This proved to be extremely popular and steadily evolved through various eye-shaped, lozenge-shaped, and shaped oval cross sections.

By the 1790s the 'straight' sides started to become slightly bulbous and developed various bulbous horizontal bands. In turn in the early 1800s the form became oblong and by 1805/10 acquired ball feet. At the same time silver handles with ivory insulators rapidly became fashionable.

The early 1800s also saw the introduction of

12. Oblong bulbous, first quarter 19th century. This example by Paul Storr is much heavier than the norm which were usually quite light.
Christie's New York

13. Regency, first quarter 19th century. Top quality by Paul Storr. The design is based on a classic oil lamp.
Christie's New York

a new shape based on a classic oil lamp. This low broad shape is arguably the ideal for making a good cup of tea. (Always remember with teapots that the taller the pot the worse it is, the narrower the pot, the worse it is).

The 'rounded' version of this type evolved steadily through to the mid-nineteenth century with the 'melon' shape being particularly popular.

By the second quarter of the nineteenth century earlier forms started to be copied and/or interpreted. Particularly popular from the 1870s/'80s onwards was the revival of the late eighteenth century oval straight-sided form. Most are easily distinguished from the originals by virtue of their sides tapering slightly, a feature which will not be found on the originals.

By the end of the nineteenth century the so-called 'Queen Anne' style was most popular and continued to be so well into the twentieth

14. Melon, second quarter 19th century. This example shows nicely its development from the slightly earlier plain compressed spherical.
Sotheby's

century. It is based largely on the late eighteenth/early nineteenth century slightly bulbous oval form and has a lobed lower half to the body.

The 1920s/'30s saw the development of various Art Deco forms. Since the end of World War Two, with the exception of some very exciting designs by some of the modern artist craftsmen goldsmiths, most examples have been rather slavish reproductions of eighteenth and early nineteenth century designs.

Pitfalls

It is particularly important to examine teapots very carefully for signs of wear and tear. You only have to think of what a teapot has to go through every time you make a pot of tea to realise why. Many a tea and coffee service will have the coffee pot, sugar and cream in first class condition but the teapot will be worn out.

Examine carefully the hinges, handle sockets and spout for signs of splits, old repairs etc. Also look for repairs to the body and check that there are no leaks.

Quality

Flush hinges usually indicate a well-made pot. It is much easier to 'sit' a hinge on a pot.

15. (Above) Mid-19th century. Based on the 1770s drum (see No. 9), but easy to distinguish with its tapering slightly incurved body and tuck-in base. Sotheby's

16. (Left) Last quarter 19th century/very early 20th. Not to be confused with the 18th century shaped oval on which it is based (see No. 11). Notice the tapering body which you never get with the original. Christie's New York

17. 'Queen Anne', late 19th/early 20th century. Made in huge quantities. Apart from the name it has nothing to do with Queen Anne at all. It is nearest in design to the oval bulbous pots of the very late 18th/very early 19th century. Christie's South Kensington

1. Late 17th/early 18th century. The pull-off lid was used to measure the tea.   Sotheby's

2. Canted oblong, first quarter 18th century. The whole top section slides out horizontally.   Sotheby's

TEA CADDIES/CANISTERS

First found at the end of the seventeenth century, the name caddy is a corruption of the Malay word *cati* which was a weight (1⅛ lb – 0.5kg) by which tea was first purchased.

As with teapots early examples are small because of the very high cost of tea.

Late seventeenth/early eighteenth century examples are usually of oblong shape with a pull-off cylindrical lid (No. 1) which was used as the measure for the tea.

This early form develops as the eighteenth century progresses. Variations of the basic shape become the norm. The construction also

3. Bulbous, oblong, mid-18th century pair of tea caddies and a sugar box. These are London 1748 by Thomas Heming. The Chinese figures and architecture within the rococo foliate scrollwork add significantly to the value.   Sotheby's

4. (Far left) Oblong, 1770/80. The decoration is from textile designs of the period. Notice the key-hole – many caddies were locked, tea being very expensive. Sotheby's

5. (Left) Tea chest form, 1770s. Notice the engraved Chinese characters. Sotheby's

changes, the base or the top being made so as to be detachable, usually sliding out to one side. This enabled a lead liner to be inserted. Occasionally these are still present.

By the mid-eighteenth century larger bulbous oblong as well as round baluster examples were most popular. In most cases these will be chased with rococo decoration.

From about 1770 onwards, with the introduction of the drum shape, caddies follow, for the most part, the shapes of teapots. (A notable exception is the tea chest form, No. 5). By this period, with the reduction in the price of tea leading to increased consumption, much larger caddies are found.

The popularity of the use of silver for caddies declined in the nineteenth century. Examples are quite difficult to find until a revival in the late nineteenth/early twentieth century when a great many were produced. These are usually based on earlier designs and are mostly of small size again.

For some time there was much debate over the use of the third piece, either 'caddy' or bowl, normally found within a cased set. The accepted explanation was that it was for your own blend produced from the green and black tea kept in the other two caddies. With the discovery of the Wakelin ledgers (and subsequently other contemporary documentary evidence), the problem was solved. Always in the ledgers the entry will be for a pair of tea canisters and a sugar box (or a sugar bowl). There should no longer be any debate.

When a sugar box is present it will normally be slightly larger than the caddies. If the caddies are of oblong cross section the sugar box will usually be square.

6. Neo-classic, shaped oval, last quarter 18th century. Now made to match the teapot. Sotheby's

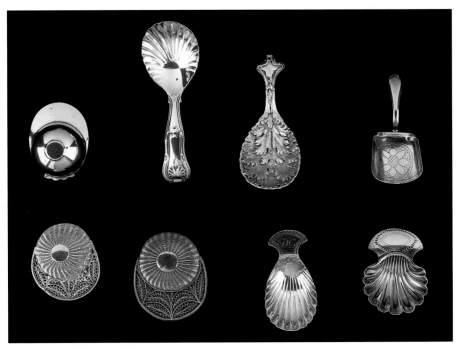

1. This selection gives some idea of the enormous variety to be found. Christie's New York

CADDY SPOONS

A long established area of collecting (there is even a specialist collectors' society) and, as a result, a more difficult area for a new collector to get into.

The earliest accepted examples date from about 1770. Their production increased steadily until the end of the century and then took off in a big way through the first half of the nineteenth century

All the conventional flatware patterns of the period are of course to be found. It is, however, for the most part, all the other designs that interest collectors.

Birmingham was the greatest centre of production and it is there that most of the 'novelty' forms were produced – jockey caps, eagles' wings, hands, fish, tea leaves and vine leaves, to name but a few.

By the second half of the nineteenth century production was in decline.

Pitfalls

Forgery is a problem, even with straight-forward designs.

The most common fakes are made by cutting off the hallmarked end of a teaspoon handle and soldering a caddy spoon bowl on to this shortened stem. Shovel-shaped examples are often faked this way – genuine examples should be marked on the shovel itself, not the handle.

Jockey caps in particular have been made out of hallmarked, scrap, watch cases of the early nineteenth century. The lack of a duty mark (watch cases were exempt) and the use of an incuse punch for the maker's mark will normally give the game away. (Incuse – the letters only are stamped into the surface; they have no surrounding punch; this type of maker's mark was used extensively by watchmakers.)

1. Sugar box, 17th century.
Only occasionally found, this
one dates from 1661.
Sotheby's

SUGAR BOWLS, BASINS AND BOXES
Up to the end of the seventeenth century sugar would normally have been kept in a box (No. 1).

Sugar bowls are first found, with the increasingly rapid spread of tea drinking, from the late seventeenth century onwards. Boxes continue but are now made to match tea caddies, forming part of the cased set of a pair of tea caddies and a sugar box (Tea Caddies No. 3, page 79) or a sugar bowl (No. 4). It is clear from contemporary records that their use with the caddies was for sugar.

Although many bowls or basins from the first half of the eighteenth century have no lid today, most were originally supplied with

2. Sugar bowl and cover, first half 18th century. The standard English design. Octagonal examples are much sought after. The lid was probably used as a spoon dish.   Sotheby's

3. Panel sides, first half 18h century. There is much dispute as to the use of these once over about 6in. (15cm) diameter (sugar, slops, rinsing have all been suggested). Small examples are accepted as for sugar.   Sotheby's

4. Bowl and cover with tea caddies, mid-18th century. This superb set, all in a fitted case, was made in London in 1748 by James Shruder. The caddies are of oblong cross section. Had a box been ordered instead of a bowl for the sugar it would normally have been of square cross section.
Sotheby's

them. The lids are quite distinctive, having a rim foot instead of a central finial (No. 2). It is believed that this was to enable the lid to be used as a stand for the teaspoons. Sizes in the order of 4in. (10cm) diameter are normal.

By the mid-eighteenth century, as the fashion for using spoon dishes declined, so the lids lose their rim foot and acquire a finial (No. 4). Some clearly did not have lids (No. 3).

In Scotland and in Ireland a distinctive

5. *Scottish sugar bowl, 18th century. The everted lip is quite distinctive. If Irish it would be more likely to be on three legs.* Sotheby's

6. *Classic swing handle (circular) basket, 1770s/'80s. Always examine the piercing for splits and repairs. The handle when flat should follow the line of the top edge.* Christie's South Kensington

variation of the standard hemispherical bowl is found. These have an everted lip (No. 5) which is only very rarely found in England. Most Scottish examples stand on a circular foot and are plain. In Ireland most stand on three feet (often lion mask) and are chased.

By the 1770s the tall circular 'classic vase' became popular (No. 6). These, which are normally referred to as baskets, have a swing handle and, when pierced (as most are), have a glass liner. The oval quickly superseded this and dominated the late eighteenth century (No. 7).

Both circular and oval swing handle examples are found in two sizes (with the oval one of about 6in to 7in – 15cm to 18cm – width and the other about 5in. to 6in. – 13cm to 15cm) which if you are lucky will be found as a pair. These can be confusing. The larger one is for sugar and the smaller one for cream (which was ladled out).

From the early nineteenth century sugars were designed as part of tea/coffee services (see page 88) and only rarely exhibit any individual design.

7. *Classic swing handle (oval) baskets, 1780s/'90s. Obviously not a pair but showing clearly the difference in size between sugar and cream baskets. (Cream 4½in. – 11.5cm – wide, sugar 6in. – 15cm – wide.)* Sotheby's

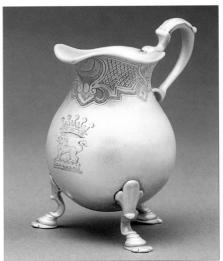

CREAM/MILK JUGS

These developed from the early eighteenth century with the increasing popularity of tea.

Early eighteenth century examples are, with only rare exceptions, of pitcher (sometimes known as sparrow beak) form. These stand on a low foot (No. 1). They developed into the three-legged pear-shaped jugs of the mid-eighteenth century (No. 2 and 3) which in turn acquired a drop bottom and usually stands on a central spreading foot by the 1760/70 period (No. 8).

Classic vase-shaped examples steadily replaced the earlier forms during the 1770s. The earliest of these normally have their circular foot standing on a square pedestal (No. 9). The pedestal in turn disappears during the 1780s (No. 10).

1. (Above left) Pitcher or sparrow beak, Queen Anne to early George II. If octagonal then highly sought after. Sotheby's

2. (Above right) Pear-shaped on three feet, mid-18th century. This example of 1732 is by Paul de Lamerie. Christie's New York

3. (Right centre) Pear-shaped on three feet, mid-18th century. Standard type of which many were made. Usually quite light. If decorated ensure that it is original. Sotheby's

4. (Right) Helmet on three feet, mid-18th century. Characteristically Irish. If on a pedestal foot it should be early. Christie's New York

5. (Above) Milk boat, mid-18th century. A very distinctive Scottish form. Easily mistaken for a sauce boat (which will be deeper). Sotheby's

6. (Right) Cream jug, mid-18th century, Pear-shaped on spreading foot. The same basic form as No. 3. Christie's New York

To understand the form which first appears in the late 1790s it is easiest to imagine cutting the earlier form in half horizontally (Nos. 10 and 11).

From here on the majority of cream jugs are made as part of a tea/coffee service with the design based on the teapot (see Tea/Coffee Services, page 88).

Other forms

Lidded oviform or egg-shaped examples standing on three legs may sometimes be found from the first half of the eighteenth century. Most were made by Huguenot goldsmiths.

Since they are both rare and much sought after, prices for good examples will be high.

A distinctive and unique form was produced in Scotland in the mid-18th century (No. 5). These are often mistaken for sauce boats,

7. Cow creamer, mid-18th century. Nearly all (if 18th century) are by John Schuppe. Christie's New York

8. Pear shape with drop bottom, 3rd quarter 18th century. The same form is also found on three legs. This example is American (Massachusetts c.1780). Christie's New York

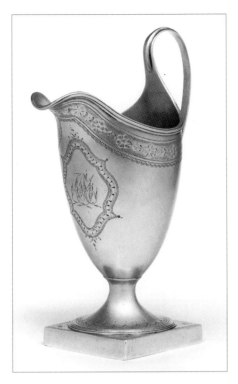

9. *Classic vase shape on square pedestal. This example was made by Peter & Jonathan Bateman.*
Private collection

which they closely resemble, but they are however much shallower.

Cow creamers (No. 7) were first produced in the 1740s by John Schuppe (who appears to have made little else). Originals are very scarce, desirable and expensive. Most that come on to the market are reproductions made in the late nineteenth/early twentieth century.

Pitfalls

Forgeries of the pitcher forms are not uncommon. These are usually made by adding a handle and a lip to the body of a baluster pepper caster (much more common and less valuable – particularly if the top is badly damaged).

Always examine handles and feet very carefully for splits and repairs. Look also (especially with three-legged examples) to see if the foot/feet have been pushed into the body.

Examine mid-eighteenth century cut edge examples for splits and repairs to the edge. This is a very common problem with this type of jug.

10. *(Left) Neo-classic, 1790s. It is easy to see from this jug how the next form was arrived at. Simply take away the body and foot below the 'central' girdle and compare with No. 11.* Sotheby's

11. *(Above) Turn of 18th/19th century. The origin of this shape is easy to see – just cut No. 10 horizontally in half.*

1. Cream boat, mid-18th century. This one by Paul de Lamerie.   Christie's New York

CREAM BOATS

Dating from the mid-eighteenth century, these are of sauce boat shape and proportion but are much smaller. Most have a cut edge.

Pitfalls

Conversions from pap-boats. This is done by simply soldering on feet and a handle. The proportions will be wrong, pap boats being much shallower (do not confuse these with the larger Scottish milk boats).

TEA/COFFEE SERVICES

The concept of a matching tea/coffee service is a comparatively modern one. Although a handful of early and mid-eighteenth century examples are known, the idea did not start to become popular until the 1780s for teasets, coffee being added to the set at the very end of the century.

Before the late eighteenth century families would acquire the necessary pieces a bit at a time and did not worry as to whether they matched or not.

The Scots appear to have been the most advanced over the idea of sets, with sets and part sets surviving from earlier in the eighteenth century.

Almost invariably the teapot was the piece around which the rest of the set was based. It is also the teapot which should always be examined first when looking at any set. It normally has a much harder life than any of the other pieces and is often worn out long before the others.

If you decide to assemble a service always acquire the teapot first and match the other pieces to it. Remember also to choose a design that can be found reasonably easily.

Early tea services (1780/'90s) often comprise

1. Neo-classic, late 18th century. Although all matching, each piece is by a different maker. In such cases always question whether the set is a modern marriage which has been engraved recently to match. Genuine original mixes are not unusual.
                                                                              Sotheby's

2. Bulbous oval, c.1800. Greater harmony by this date as the concept of the service becomes finally established as the norm.
Sotheby's

3. Regency oblong bulbous. Produced and surviving in large quantities.
Christie's
New York

4. Regency compressed spherical. The majority of this form are normally of better quality (heavier, etc.) than most of the oblong bulbous examples (No. 3).
Sotheby's

5. (Above) Second quarter 19th century. This could almost be called the Barnard pattern since it would be surprising to find this design by anyone else. Many sets and part sets survive – a good one if you want to build a service. This example of 1834/5 is more unusual, having leaf decoration on alternate panels.
Christie's New York

6. (Above) Victorian, mid-19th century. What can you say? It has great character. Someone, somewhere, has and will love it.
Sotheby's

7. (Right) Victorian 'Gothic', mid-19th century. It is always a plus to find a set in its original case. Many sets, as this one, have presentation inscriptions. They are part of the history of the piece and should never be removed.
Sotheby's

8. French, 19th century. A very popular design throughout those areas of Europe most directly influenced by French design. Phillips

9. Aesthetic Movement, 1870s, parcel gilt. A set of small size showing the Japanese influence at this time. In the late 19th/early 20th century such small sets with porcelain cups etc., all in a fitted case, became popular. (The silver is by Elkington, the porcelain Royal Worcester.) Sotheby's

10. 'Classic Revival', late 19th/early 20th century. Variations of this design were produced in huge quantities, particularly in electroplate and electro-plated Britannia metal. Sotheby's

11. 'Queen Anne', late 19th/early 20th century. This design rivalled if not exceeded the popularity of No. 10. Unlike this example, most are plain above the lobing on the body.   Christie's South Kensington

12. China Trade, late 19th/early 20th century. A good many sets were produced in the trading ports – Hong Kong, Shanghai, etc., for the European market. These are becoming increasingly sought after. The quality is always good.   Christie's South Kensington

a teapot (with or without stand) and two swing-handled baskets, one larger than the other. In such a case the larger of the baskets was for sugar and the smaller for milk or cream. Cream baskets were popular at the time and followed on from the cream pails of the mid-eighteenth century. In both cases a ladle was used for the cream.

Salvers/Trays/Spoon Dishes/Spoon Trays

1. Footed salver, first half 17th century. Any examples of this date are rare. Sotheby's

2. (Above) Footed salver, Charles II. Standard form with its original two-handled cup and cover.

Sotheby's

3. (Left) Octafoil salver, mostly late Queen Anne/early George II. Not easy to find, highly desirable. Christie's New York

SALVERS

Terminology

As a general guide if it has handles then it is a tray. If not (regardless of size), it is a salver which if small – up to about 6in. or 7in. (15 or 18cm) – may alternatively be described as a waiter.

Tazza is a nineteenth century misnomer often used to describe a salver on a central foot. These were in fact the original salvers. They were produced into the first half of the eighteenth century at which time small salvers

were referred to as waiters or hand waiters. Large salvers were called 'Tables' and would in many cases originally have been provided with a wooden table support. Most, sadly, have long since parted company.

Development

Anything other than a circular form for the early salver on central foot would be exceptionally rare – if genuine. Size varies enormously. In the seventeenth century they

4. Square, mostly first half 18th century (the oblong version is very rare). This example is by Paul de Lamerie.   Sotheby's

5. Shaped square, usually early George II.
                                          Sotheby's

6. Shaped circular (Bath), second quarter 18th century. The superb seal engraving would put this example way beyond most people's reach. Sotheby's

7. Mid-18th century rococo. This is about as rococo as most salver borders got.   Sotheby's

were often made *en suite* with two-handled cups for which they formed the stand.

Pitfalls
Edges should be carefully examined for splits and repairs. Repairs are often difficult.

Always check a salver by viewing it edge on for any distortion. Warping can be very difficult to correct.

Feet should be checked for splits and repairs.

The centre should be examined for signs of removal of arms, initials, etc., and re-engraving.

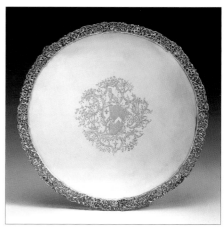

8. *Mid-18th century rococo. Only rarely will a rococo salver of asymmetric shape be found.*

Christie's New York

9. *Openwork border. Cast openwork borders when found are usually of mid-18th century date.*

Sotheby's

10. *(Above left) Adam oval, last quarter 18th century. A particularly desirable shape.*

Christie's New York

11. *(Above) Adam circular, last quarter 18h century. The most usual shape at this period. This example has a pierced border which (if in good condition) will add to its value.* Christie's New York

12. *(Left) Regency oblong. Less common than circular examples at this period. Very small examples were teapot stands.* Christie's New York

95

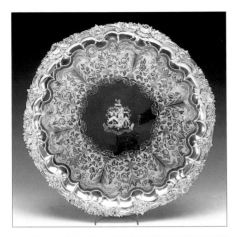

13. (Left) 19th century rococo revival. The majority of 19th century examples are copies or interpretations of 18th century designs.   Sotheby's

14. (Left below) Kettle stand. This distinctive form was used particularly by Paul de Lamerie for his kettle stands.   Sotheby's

It is a common problem with salvers. An examination of the back of the salver will often reveal the signs of this.

Patches are not uncommon but are usually pretty obvious.

Many salvers have thin centres where engravings have been removed.

Footed salvers are particularly vulnerable to splits forming where the foot joins the body. Look out for these as well as repairs. Plates are sometimes added between the foot and the body to strengthen an otherwise weak centre.

TRAYS

Only rarely encountered before the second half of the eighteenth century. Early examples (i.e. before the 1760s) seem to have been soup tureen stands, examples of which survive *en suite.*

The concept of the tea tray appears to have developed in the late eighteenth century. This resulted from the switch away from a lady preparing the tea herself at the tea table to tea being prepared in the kitchen and brought in already made. (It is interesting to see how

1. Adam, oval, late 18th century (London 1795).
Christie's New York

15. Kettle on stand. Any 18th century 'salver' of triangular form will have been made as a kettle stand.

Christie's New York

2. Regency oval. A superb example with cast open-work border by Benjamin Smith (London 1804).
Christie's New York

3. Regency shaped oval. This form continued to develop through the 19th century. This example is by Paul Storr, London 1814.
Christie's New York

4. 19th century shaped oblong. Developing in the early 19th century, the oblong form, with its many borders and surface decorations, has been produced ever since.
Christie's New York

1. George I oblong incurved corner.   Sotheby's

scarce tea kettles, which had been common up to this time, became.)

Only rarely will English gallery trays be found before the latter part of the nineteenth century. Tens of thousands have been produced since, the bulk being electro-plated on copper. Frequently these are erroneously described as Old Sheffield plate. No such thing is known to exist.

Pitfalls

The point at which the handles join the body takes a lot of stress and not surprisingly is vulnerable to splits – look out for these or repairs of these. Examples where handles have been added to meat dishes to make them into trays may be encountered. Otherwise the pitfalls are the same as for salvers.

SPOON DISHES/SPOON TRAYS

Dating from about 1700 through to the 1730s, these small (usually oblong, oval, or shaped versions of either) dishes are easily mistaken for snuffers trays.

Distinguishing one from the other is easy. Snuffers trays of the early 18th century have handles; spoon dishes do not. An obvious danger here is a snuffers tray of the period which has had its handle removed – look for signs of solder on the back where the handle would normally have been fixed.

The practice of placing teaspoons on such a dish declined as the mid-18th century approached and so the dishes died out. (See also **Sugars** for the use of lids as spoon dishes.)

Pitfalls

As for Salvers

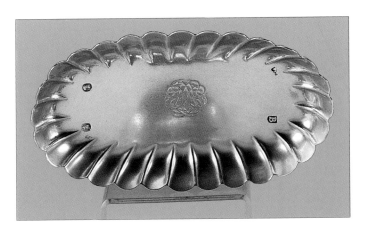

2. George I oval 'fluted'. Sotheby's

99

CHAPTER 10

Condiments
Salts/Casters/Mustard Pots

*1.Capstan/pulley salt, 17th century. This example
(one of four) is London c.1670 and 5in. (12.7cm)
diameter. Individual examples with scrolls projecting
from the top edge can be much larger. Sets of this
period are rare.*   Sotheby's

*2. Capstan, end of 17th century. Always very light
and difficult to find in good condition.*   Sotheby's

SALTS

Salts had by the end of the seventeenth century
lost their earlier importance when a principal
salt would have been placed between the host
and the most important guest at a meal. They
did, however, continue to develop along their
own quite independent line from mustards
and peppers until the end of the eighteenth
century.

Although salts survive from the fifteenth
century onwards, it is not until the capstan
form of trencher salt of the late seventeenth
century that examples become comparatively
easy to obtain. These are quickly followed at
the turn of the century by oval, circular and
lobed circular trenchers, all of which are much
lower in height.

By the 1720s the 'octagonal' trencher
dominates. From this time onwards the pedestal
form, which is usually by a top Huguenot goldsmith, may also be found.

The mid-eighteenth century sees the domi-

nance of the compressed spherical on three legs
form which is also known as the cauldron shape
(four legs are sometimes found).

Pierced openwork salts develop from the
mid-century. It is with these that glass liners
make their first appearance (openwork salts are
the only ones that require liners).

The standard form for these is straight-sided
oval on four claw ball feet. These start with
rococo pierced sides. By the 1770s neo-classic
piercing has taken over and the form has
superseded in popularity the 'cauldron' type.

During the last quarter of the eighteenth
century various classic shapes may be found of
which the 'boat' shape, either with or without
handles, was most popular. It is also from this
period onwards that gilt interiors become
standard (for examples without glass liners).

As the nineteenth century progresses an
enormous variety is produced with the
'cauldron' in particular regaining its popularity
(albeit usually of a smaller size).

3. *Circular lobed trencher, turn of 17th/18th century. Always of good, heavy quality by one of the Huguenots unless a later copy.*   Sotheby's

4. *Oblong incurved corner trencher, mostly second quarter 18th century. These vary greatly in quality – most are on the light side. Usually about 3in. (7.5cm) wide.*   Christie's New York

5. *'Pedestal', mostly second quarter 18th century, about 3in. (7.5cm) in diameter. Top quality, most often by a leading Huguenot. This is by Paul de Lamerie.*   Christie's New York

6. *'Cauldron', mid-18th century and on. Normally plain and on three feet. This has applied decoration and is on four feet, therefore it should be, and is, by a top maker – in this case Paul de Lamerie.*
Sotheby's

7. *Pierced openwork, second half 18th century.*

8. *Classic oval 'pedestal', last quarter 18th century.*

9. *Classical oval 'pedestal', 1770s. A significant step above the normal simple oval. These are by Robert Hennell, London 1776.*   Sotheby's

10. *Regency oblong, early 19th century and later. There are many variations of this type. Many heavy examples on lion mask feet were made of electro-plated copper and are often mistaken for Old Sheffield plate – watch out.*   Christie's New York

11. *Warwick vase, early 19th century. Occasionally such examples may be found.*   Bonhams

12. *Regency, silver gilt, 'triton holding a shell'. This is a very important salt. Probably designed by Thead and made by Paul Storr for Rundell, Bridge & Rundell. 4½in. (11.5cm)wide.*   Sotheby's

13. *19th century. Many variations of the 'cauldron' form were produced during this period, ranging from straight copies of the 18th century examples to the rococo revival interpretation illustrated.*   Sotheby's

102

14. Figure salts, mid-19th century, 6¼in. (15.9cm) high. Based on 18th century street vendors, these are highly desirable and valuable. They were made by Hunt & Roskell of London in 1855.   Sotheby's

Pitfalls

Corrosion due to the salt being left in the piece is common (see **Care, Cleaning and Conservation,** page 175).

With the 'cauldron' type the legs have often been pushed into the body. Such damage is difficult and expensive to repair.

Legs are often either repaired, split or broken. This applies particularly to the oval straight-sided form and the 'cauldron' type.

CASTERS
Sugar, Pepper, Pepperettes, Mustard,
Muffineers/Bun Peppers,
Kitchen Peppers, Pepper Mills

Sets of casters comprising a sugar, pepper and mustard were being produced by the second half of the seventeenth century. Of 'lighthouse' form, these have a bayonet fitting top (No. 1).

Distinguishing the three within a set was easy. The largest was for sugar. Although the two smaller ones are of the same size as each other, originally only the pepper was pierced.

Today the unpierced or 'blind' mustard caster is rare since most were pierced after

1. Lighthouse, last quarter 17th century. This example Edinburgh 1696 with bayonet fitting.   Sotheby's

3. *Octagonal baluster, early 18th century. A comparatively rare shape with early sleeve fitting to the lid.* Sotheby's

2. Pear, first quarter 18th century. This set is remarkable (possibly unique) with seven casters in three sizes. Made in 1705 by Joseph Ward of London. Notice the continuing use of the bayonet fitting. Sotheby's

1760. This was because the fashion, in England, changed around 1760 from serving dry mustard power, which was ladled out of the caster, to serving already made up mustard.

During the mid-eighteenth century, and sometimes earlier, sets were usually held in a frame together with an oil and vinegar bottle. These are frequently referred to as Warwick cruets (Nos. 4 and 5).

Early in the eighteenth century the bayonet was superseded by the sleeve fitting for the tops (No. 3).

By the turn of the seventeenth/eighteenth century a rather chunky pear shape was in favour (No. 2), which by the late Queen Anne/ George I period is of a more slender form and is normally octagonal.

The vase shape dominates the mid-18th century and is found mostly of circular or octagonal form. A particularly fine variation of the latter has alternately straight and incurved panels (Nos. 6, 7, and 8).

By the third quarter of the century the baluster form is the most common (Nos. 9 and 10).

Radical changes occurred around the 1760s. Mustard casters were replaced by mustard pots (see page 109). Sugar casters fell out of fashion in favour of using sifter spoons and pepper pots

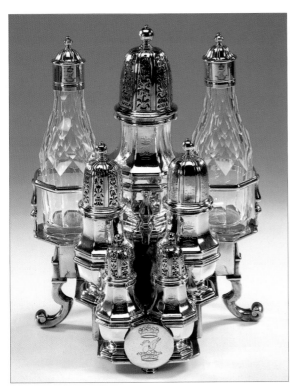

4. Warwick cruet with octagonal vase-shaped casters. Made in 1715
by Anthony Nelme of London and at one time in the Warwick Castle
collection, it is believed to be the example from which the name
originated. (see No. 5 for the more conventional form.) Notice the
'blind' mustard.   Sotheby's

(now of smaller size) became part of the
developing concept of the 'condiment' set.

Casters of smaller size (3in. to 3½in. – 7.5cm
to 9cm) of the first half of the eighteenth
century (and very rarely earlier) with a very
low 'dome' with the piercing on the top are
usually referred to as muffineers or (particularly if of baluster form) bun peppers.

The term 'kitchen pepper' is used to describe
examples which have a handle. Normally these
are of early eighteenth century date, of small

5. Warwick cruet, mid-18th century, with vase-shaped
casters. The standard design with three casters and
two glass bottles, all in a cinquefoil frame with central
handle.   Sotheby's

7 (Far left). Octagonal vase, mostly George I and early George II. This example (part of a set) is superb – top quality work, top maker – Anne Tanqueray, and, engraved with original royal arms. What more could be asked? Sotheby's

8 (Left) Vase shape, usually mid-18th century. The standard design of this period made in large numbers in London by Samuel Wood. This example is significantly more desirable and valuable, having been made in America (Milford, Connecticut) in about 1785.
Christie's New York

9. (Far left) Baluster, third quarter 18th century. These usually have a plain body. When chased, as this one, make sure the decoration is original (this one is). Sotheby's

10. (Left) Baluster, last quarter 18th century. By this date they are usually quite light and have a more 'spindly' appearance than No. 9. Notice that the piercing is just a series of holes drilled without much care and the decoration is engraved in much the same way. Not a distinguished piece of silver but typical of a late 18th century mass-produced piece. The maker – Hester Bateman. Sotheby's

11 (Above). Cruet, third quarter 18th century. Based on the Warwick cruet, but with silver mounted cut-glass bodies. For obvious reasons not many have survived with all the original glass. How original everything is will make a very big difference to the value. Sotheby's

12. (Top left) Classic vase, last quarter 18th century and on. Normally of small size. Sometimes with a pierced body and glass liner. Private collection

13. (Left, centre) Second half 19th century. The design is based on a form of German beaker. Private collection

14. (Left) Owl, mid-19th century. Much sought after novelty form. Christie's South Kensington

size, and are straight sided (either circular or octagonal (No. 17)).

Pepperettes (small pepper pots) became very popular in the late nineteenth/early twentieth century. An enormous variety of novelty forms were produced: owls, milk churns, chauffeurs, twelve bore cartridges and 'wooden' horses are all to be found alongside miniature versions of

15 (Far left). Milk churn, second half 19th century. Novelty pepper.
Christie's South Kensington

16. (Left) Lighthouse caster, 19th/early 20th century. Many sugar casters based on this 17th century design (see No. 1) were made at this time. Their decoration, and often their proportions, give their date away. Some, usually with leaf floral and foliate chasing, have screw-on tops.
Christie's South Kensington

conventional eighteenth century caster forms (Nos. 12-15).

Pepper mills or grinders make their first appearance in the latter part of the nineteenth century. The capstan form dominates. Many are made of wood or ivory with silver mounts. Cut glass may also be found (Nos. 18 and 19).

Pitfalls

The most common is with badly repaired splits between the piercing. Some examples have sleeves soldered into the top to restrict the amount of piercing or to strengthen a damaged top. Both are best avoided unless the price is very reasonable and all you want is a working example. (Detachable interior restrictors are perfectly acceptable.)

Pepper mills are subject to a lot of stress when in use. Always ensure that the mechanism if working properly.

17 (Above left). Kitchen pepper, early 18th century. The engraving which commemorates the coronation of Queen Anne adds greatly to this one.   Sotheby's

18 (Above right). Pepper mill, late 19th century and on. Capstan in silver-mounted wood.   Christie's South Kensington

19 (Right). Pepper mill, turn of 19th/20th century. Silver-mounted glass. Private collection

20 (Far right). Pepper mill, turn of 19th/20th century. An unusual novelty example formed as a champagne cork.   Private collection

2. *Pierced drum mustard of the 1760s. The earliest form normally found.*   Private Collection

1. *Mustard caster. These with no piercing are known as blind casters and may occasionally be found up to the 1760s. This example is particularly rare, being Scottish.*   Private Collection

MUSTARD POTS
(see also Casters above)

Although some extremely rare earlier examples may be found, the idea of serving made-up mustard in a pot really developed in England from the early 1760s. Prior to this mustard powder was served in a blind caster (No. 1).

The earliest are of drum shape with a flat lid, a solid base and, usually, pierced sides. These are followed very quickly by examples with the base cut out to enable easier removal of the glass liner.

The pattern of development of shape then follows very closely that of teapots – drum, oval straight sides, classic vase, oval bulbous sides, oblong bulbous, compressed spherical and melon.

By the early nineteenth century a drum of rather squatter shape is to be found as well as a compressed spherical form on three legs which

3. *Classic vase-shaped mustard. This is the less common form of the last quarter of the 18th century.*   Private Collection

follows the form of eighteenth century cauldron-shaped salt cellars.

As the nineteenth century progresses many novelty forms were produced – owls, baskets, Mr. Punch, monkeys, cats and even a kangaroo, a busby, and a drum are all to be found.

Many reproductions of eighteenth century

4. Late Regency/Early Victorian. With scenes after Teniers this type is particularly associated with Edward Farrell of London. Private Collection

5. These mid-19th century representations of the drum mustard are associated with the Fox family of goldsmiths in London. Private Collection

6. An unusual and rare novelty egg mustard pot of the second half of the 19th century. Private Collection

7. A Victorian interpretation of the late 18th century pierced straight-sided oval form. Private Collection

8. A very unusual Aesthetic Movement example from the last quarter of the 19th century. Private Collection

examples have been produced since the late nineteenth century. These are most often of a smaller size than the originals.

Pitfalls
Small mugs which have been converted into mustard pots by the addition of a lid are a danger.

CHAPTER 11

Drinking Vessels
Beakers/Cups (Two-Handled)/Goblets/Porringers
Quaichs/Stirrup Cups/Tankards/Mugs

1. 17th century, engraved.   Sotheby's

2. 17th century, chased.   Sotheby's

BEAKERS

A very ancient vessel. These derive from the cut-off (wide) end of an ox horn. British examples (Nos. 1, 2 and 3), up to the late seventeenth century, usually have flared sides. Straight-sided examples are found after this (No. 4).

Beakers were very popular in Scandinavia where a very much more flared form is found (No. 6).

Some of the greatest are the superbly engraved examples made in the Netherlands during the seventeenth century (No. 5).

3. Late 17th century. The superb engraving adds greatly to this example.   Sotheby's

4. Late 18th century from Malta. Sotheby's

Pitfalls

Splits or repaired splits to the top edge. Be very wary of Elizabethan and some seventeenth century examples. Many communion cups have had their stem and foot removed. Look for signs of solder on the base.

5. 17th century. Engraved beakers of this form were produced particularly in Germany and the Low Countries. Christie's New York

6. Scandinavian. Notice the strongly flared shape so typical of this area. (This example Swedish, mid-18th century.) Some of these can be very large.
Christie's New York

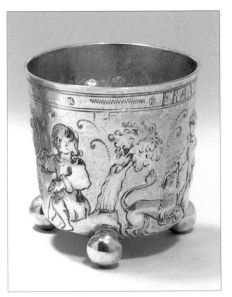

7. 17th/18th century. Examples on three ball feet are usually German (this one Augsburg, late 17th century). The design was often modified to form a mug in England in the 19th century.

Christie's New York

8. French form. Most examples date from the late 17th century and on through the 18th century. Usually about 4½in. (11.5cm) high. Sotheby's

9. German 16th century 'nesting beaker' form. Squatter than the French (see No. 8). Fine copies of these were made in England in the early 19th century. Sotheby's

*1. Pair of 1691
college or ox-eye
cups, 4in. (10cm)
high.* Sotheby's

*2. Common-
wealth silver gilt
lidded example
of 1656.4½in.
(11.5cm) high.*
Sotheby's

*3. Charles II ogee-shaped cup with typical floral
chasing, London 1662. 5¾in. (14.5cm) high.*

Bonhams

CUPS (TWO-HANDLED)

Apart from extremely rare sixteenth century
examples it is with the ox-eye or college cup of
the seventeenth century that it is best to start.
The name derives from the shape of the handles
and the fact that most surviving examples
belong to collegiate bodies.

The vast majority of seventeenth century
cups, however, have either a straight-sided body
with tuck-in base or an ogee-shaped body (any
other shape is scarce/rare). In both cases handles
of S scroll shape are the norm. It was normal for
the medium to larger scale examples to have a
lid. Decoration is extremely diverse and largely
dependent on date.

There is often debate over the correct name
to use – caudle cup and porringer being the

4. A very standard Charles II example. Formal chased acanthus leaves were popular in the 1670s. 1676. 6½in. (16.5cm) high. Sotheby's

5. William and Mary example with the chinoiserie flat chased decoration so popular in the 1680s. 1689. 6¾in. (17cm) high. Sotheby's

6. c.1700. Notice the domed lid and more curved base when compared to the previous example. Sotheby's

8. By 1715 the body is taller and the handles often have an extra scroll at the top (particularly when made by a Huguenot). Moulded girdles are now a feature. Sotheby's

7. Cups of this form were made in very large numbers at the turn of the 17th/18th century. The basic type with slight modification was still being made as late as the 1760s. Bonhams

9. Increasingly elaborate applied decoration is typical of the 1730s.   Sotheby's

9. Increasingly elaborate applied decoration is typical of the 1730s.   Sotheby's

most popular. I would suggest that the best answer is simply to refer to them as two-handled cups – nobody could argue with that. (For the true porringer, see page 120.)

An important change took place at the turn of the seventeenth/eighteenth century. With the developments in glass at this time it began to replace silver as the principal material for drinking vessels in the upper levels of society. As a result, silver two-handled cups start to develop more as presentation and display pieces rather than practical drinking vessels. This can clearly be seen as they increase in size and the

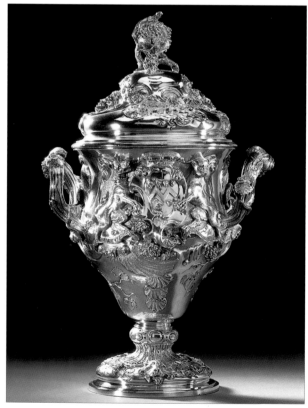

10. A superb rococo example of 1742 by Paul de Lamerie. Notice how even the handles are asymmetric.
Christie's New York

designs become less functional. The end result is, of course, the 'trophy cup'.

Pitfalls
Look for splits and repairs where handles join the body. With seventeenth century and later examples look carefully for holes and/or repairs in the high points of any chasing. These are very common problems.

11. (Above, left) A rare early Old Sheffield plate example of about 1765. Notice the drop bottom so typical of the period. Private collection

12. (Above) Neo-classic silver gilt cup on plinth by Paul Storr, London 1795/1799. Sotheby's

13. (Left) Regency campagna shape. Most cups were now for presentation. Unusually it has its original case. 1810. 15½in. (39.25cm) high. Sotheby's

117

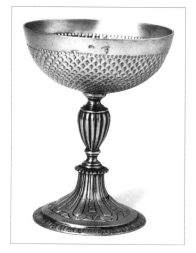

1. and 2. (Above and centre) Elizabethan/early 17th century wine cups.
Sotheby's

3. Communion cup.   Sotheby's

GOBLETS/WINE CUPS

The great period for these was up to the end of the seventeenth century. It was with the increasing use of glass that their popularity declined at this time. They enjoyed something of a revival in the late eighteenth century when pairs became quite popular. During the nineteenth century they were often made to match claret jugs. Increasingly, however, at this time they were made as trophies.

Elizabethan/early seventeenth century examples usually have either a deep conical or a shallow 'hemispherical' bowl. In both cases these are on a slender tapering stem standing on a concave foot. Most are heavily decorated (Nos. 1 and 2).

In the first half of the seventeenth century the bucket-shaped bowl on baluster stem becomes standard. These normally quite plain cups have been much reproduced this century (Nos. 4, 5 and 6).

In the mid-seventeenth century a small (about 4 to 5in., 10 to 12.5cm high) very crude form was popular. These retain the bucket shape for the bowl but have a trumpet-shaped

4. First quarter of the 17th century.   Sotheby's

118

5 and 6. (Above and centre) Second quarter to second half of the   *7. Mid-17th century.*   Sotheby's
17th century.   Sotheby's

8. 1760-1770.   Sotheby's   *9 and 10. Late 18th century.*   Sotheby's

foot. This spreads directly from the base of the bowl with no intervening stem. Decoration is nearly always a combination of simple flat chasing and matting (No. 7).

Most late eighteenth century examples are of neo-classical vase shape (Nos. 9 and 10)

apart from a small group from the 1760s which have an almost egg-shaped bowl, spindle shaped stem and almost invariably a gadroon edge to the foot (No.8).

By the early nineteenth century the classic campagna shape was the norm for the bowl

11. First half of the 19th century.

Sotheby's

*12. Second half of the 19th
century.* Sotheby's

(No. 11). This was followed in the mid-nineteenth century by a wide variety (as would be expected at this time). However, by far the most common was a version of the late eighteenth century classic form but now with a more slender stem (No. 12).

Pitfalls

Splits to the top edge and/or the junction of stem with bowl and/or foot. A common problem is where the stem has been crushed into the foot and/or bowl.

It is quite usual to find early communion cups being sold as secular wine cups (they sell better that way! (No. 3)).

PORRINGERS (BLEEDING BOWLS)

These shallow drinking bowls which characteristically have a single pierced flat handle are most commonly referred to as bleeding bowls. This is a nineteenth century misnomer.

Most date from the second half of the seventeenth century. Any earlier examples are very rare. A few were made in the early eighteenth century.

Pitfalls

Splits where the handle joins the body. Splits in the handle itself. (Note: handles are normally partially marked.)

1. London, 1705. Phillips

2. American. Boston c.1780 by Paul Revere.

Bonhams

QUAICHS

A uniquely Scottish form characterised by its shallow bowl and two (occasionally three) box-like handles (No.1).

Silver quaichs derived in the seventeenth century from wooden examples (No. 2). A combination of both materials with wooden bowl together with silver handles and mounts is normal. Many silver examples are engraved to simulate the earlier wooden bowls. There is a wide size range.

They are still made today and are particularly popular as christening presents in Scotland.

Pitfalls

Any damage to the handles is difficult and expensive to repair.

STIRRUP CUPS

Formed as animal heads, usually foxes, these date from about 1760 onwards. Designed for use when seated on horseback, they do not have a foot and when in use must be held until empty.

Stags' and hunting dogs' heads may sometimes be found (usually of nineteenth century or later date).

1. (Top) Late 17th century quaich. Sotheby's

2. (Above) 17th/early 18th century silver-mounted wood quaich.
Christie's New York

Below: 19th century stirrup cups. Sotheby's

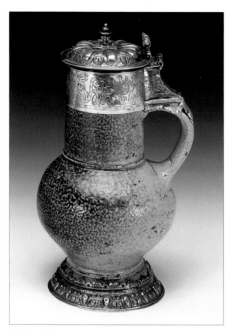

1. Elizabethan tigerware jug. A squatter version may be found from the 1550s which was sometimes made entirely of silver. A good many were mounted in the West Country, particularly, as with this example, in Exeter. Sotheby's

2. Elizabeth/James I. The tall, narrow proportions characterise the rare examples of this period. Most are heavily decorated and gilded. Sotheby's

TANKARDS

The difference between tankards and mugs is simply that tankards have lids and mugs do not – regardless of size.

Most tankards are of quart size or larger. The majority of mugs will be of pint size. Smaller examples of mugs are often referred to as christening mugs, and mostly date from the very late eighteenth century onwards.

Tankards are first found in England in the mid-sixteenth century when their shape is more akin to that of a German beer Stein (tall and narrow with a domed lid (No. 2)). Also used as a drinking vessel at this period was the tigerware jug. These were of salt-glazed

3. Mid-17th century with 'single step' to the lid. Notice the plain base, a feature of the second quarter of the 17th century. Compare with No. 5.
Christie's New York

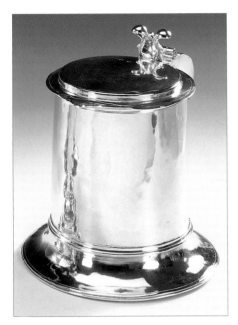

5. Second half 17th century, 'single step'. Notice the moulding at the base (compare with No. 3). During the 1680s chinoiserie decoration may be found on this type. Sotheby's

4. Mid-17th century 'skirt' tankard. The distinctive shape of the foot, which gives it its name, was used for a very short period with tankards but continued for a very long time with flagons. Sotheby's

6. A Charles II example with chased acanthus leaves to the lower body and on the lid. A common form of decoration at this time. Sotheby's

stoneware (imported from the Rhineland and Low Countries) and were mounted with silver/silver gilt in England (No. 1).

During the second quarter of the seventeenth century the lid becomes flat and the proportion of the body alters, becoming lower and broader (No. 3).

Mid-seventeenth century examples characteristically have a spreading foot (which gives them the name 'skirt tankards') and have a single step in the lid (No. 4).

The skirt disappears in the second half of the century and the lid becomes more complex with the addition by the 1680s of a convex moulding in the step. Many examples are decorated with a broad band of acanthus leaves on the lower body as well as acanthus leaves on the lid (Nos. 5, 6, and 7).

A rare Scandinavian form with more rounded edges and pomegranate feet as well as thumb piece is also found at this time (No.9). These were made in the East Coast centres – most particularly York and to a lesser extent Newcastle-upon-Tyne. (York examples by John Plummer with engraved botanical decoration are, if genuine, highly sought after.)

123

7. American of the 17th century type illustrated in Nos. 5 and 6. Notice the distinctive fine band of 'leaf' work at the base (a feature also found on Scottish examples). As in this case, which is from New York c.1750, the date may be rather later than its English equivalent. Christie's New York

8. Scottish, late 17th/early 18th century. The finial on the lid, the band of fine leaf work at the base and the construction of the thumbpiece all (when put together) point to a Scottish origin. Sotheby's

During the early eighteenth century the lid becomes domed in addition to the existing step and convex moulding. A moulded girdle about a third of the way up to the body also becomes common, and remains a common feature until dying out in the late eighteenth century (No. 10).

Mid-eighteenth century developments run parallel with coffee pots with tuck-in bases,

popular from the mid-1720s onwards, developing into the pear shape which petered out in the 1770s (No. 12).

Straight-sided tankards became reasonably popular again in the 1760/70 period. These have taller and narrower proportions than early eighteenth century examples (No. 11).

At the end of the eighteenth and in the early nineteenth century straight-sided flat-lidded examples applied with hoops and engraved staves were fashionable (No. 13). This form together with barrel-shaped examples may occasionally be found of an earlier date. (An exceptionally rare Elizabethan example recently came on to the market).

The lids of tankards are sometimes found with a central finial. Most such examples will be Scottish (No. 8), or American. Any London example will most probably be very late seventeenth century/early eighteenth century

9. Scandinavian/Baltic type produced from the mid-17th century onwards. (This example was made in Estonia c.1700.) North Sea trading influenced design in York in the 17th century and Newcastle until well into the 18th century. Sotheby's

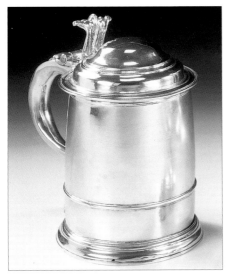

10. 18th century. This basic form with domed lid was made throughout the century. Its proportions, however, change, the body becoming narrower. Compare this early 18th century example with No. 11 which is late 18th century. Sotheby's

11. Late 18th century (in this case 1771) version of No. 10. Sotheby's

and by a Huguenot goldsmith. (Interestingly, tankards were only rarely made by the Huguenots.)

Tankards rapidly fell out of fashion during the nineteenth century. Most that were made were massive display pieces based on earlier designs (No. 14). Many eighteenth century and earlier examples were converted at this time into jugs or coffee pots and many more were chased with flowers and scrolls to make them commercially viable on the second-hand market.

Marking

A London marked tankard should have a full set of hallmarks on both the body (usually next to the handle or underneath) and the lid.

Up to the early eighteenth century it was usual for the handle to have a maker's mark (conventionally on the flat outer side about two-thirds of the way down). Sometimes the maker's mark on the handle is different from

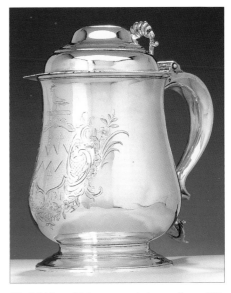

12. Mid/late 18th century baluster form. This example, which is American (New York c.1770/80) is without the moulded girdle which most have.
Christie's New York

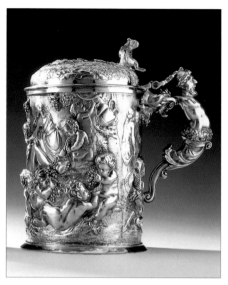

14. Regency and Victorian examples are much less common. Often made purely for display, they frequently, as with this example of 1865 by George Fox, harp back to 17th century designs.
Christie's New York

13. Most of this less common type date from the late 18th century. It became a very popular form for mugs in the late 18th/early 19th century. Sotheby's

the one on the lid and body. This usually resulted from a retailer overstamping his mark, on the lid and body, over that of the maker. This could not be done on the handle since the mark had to be struck before the handle was finally assembled. In such a case it is reasonable to assume that the mark on the handle is that of the maker and that on the body and lid the retailer. (In some cases the overstamping is quite clear.)

Pitfalls

Always look for splits and/or repairs where the handle joins the body at both the top and bottom. Similarly examine carefully the hinge and the area around.

Check for thin patches where engravings have been removed. (Sometimes this is behind the handle which has been repositioned to try to conceal the problem.) Check for de-chasing.

Always be extremely suspicious of any

decoration (the vast majority, at least 99%, of eighteenth century tankards were originally plain), other than on barrels, Charles II period acanthus leaves and very early (i.e. Elizabeth/James I) examples.

Look also for signs of where a Victorian lip/spout has been removed to restore an early tankard.

MUGS

Apart from seventeenth and nineteenth century examples these for the most part run parallel with tankards. Only rarely will they be larger than quart size. Whereas tankards effectively died out in the nineteenth century, small christening mugs became extremely popular and continued to be so into the twentieth century.

Pitfalls

As for tankards above.

1. (Top, left) Late 17th century bulbous form. The chinoiserie decoration increases its value significantly.　Sotheby's

2. (Top, right) Late 17th/early 18th century of distinctive Scottish 'thistle' shape.　Sotheby's

3. (Above, left) Late 17th/early 18th century. The moulded girdle near the top is a distinctive feature at this period.　Sotheby's

4. (Above, right) Tuck-in base, c.1720,　Sotheby's

5. (Left) Mid-18th century baluster, c.1750. This example is American by Jacob Hurd of Boston. The term can, rather than mug, is often used in America.
Christie's New York

6. *Tapered cylindrical, second half 18th century. A good many of these were made in Newcastle at this time and this is a typical example.* Sotheby's

7. *Barrel-shaped examples are more unusual. They were made over a wide period (some are very early). Most, as with this example, are from the second half of the 18th century and by good makers.* Sotheby's

8. *Most early 19th century mugs are straight sided and have reeded bands around the body. This example is more unusual with its bands of shells as well as its snake handle.* Sotheby's

9. *Mid-19th century christening mug of typical form.* Bonhams

10. The simple loop handle is typical of the late 19th/early 20th century. Engravings of nursery rhymes/children's stories add to value. Sotheby's

11. Although resembling a mug (with detachable cover), this is actually a very rare Queen Anne chocolate cup and cover of 1709. Cups of this form date from the late 17th century to the very early 18th century. Bonhams

TUMBLER CUPS

Dating from the seventeenth and eighteenth century these are raised in such a way that the base is much thicker and heavier than the rest. They should be self-righting when laid on their side.

Other than heraldic engraving, initials or inscriptions, they will nearly always be plain.

Because of their very nature there is little room for variation of form. Broadly, however, seventeenth century examples tend to be wider and shallower than those from the eighteenth century.

Pitfalls
Splits to the edge.

1. Late 17th/early 18th century. The contemporary armorial adds to the example. Sotheby's

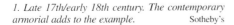

129

CHAPTER 12

Boxes

SNUFF BOXES

By the mid-eighteenth century these were being produced in large numbers in many parts of Europe with France and Germany making most of the greatest examples.

To work successfully a snuff box must be snuff-proof (snuff being a very fine powder), i.e. it must be constructed in such a way that snuff will not leak out. This is usually achieved by the combination of a fine (snuff-proof) hinge and the lid fitting tightly over a bezel (the strip of silver over which the lid fits).

Many of the earliest examples (late seventeenth/early eighteenth century) are of tortoiseshell with silver mounts and inlays Nos. 1 and 2).

Silver mounted hardstone boxes were particularly popular in the mid-eighteenth century with escutcheon shapes predominating – circular forms were also popular. Those that have silver rather than hardstone lids are mostly decorated in rococo style with romantic scenes in low relief. Many (during this period) will have a maker's mark only (No. 4).

1. Oblong, late 17th century. Tortoiseshell with silver inlay and mounts. This example is particularly desirable because of the Jacobite decoration. (Any mark would be exceptional.) Bonhams

2. Oval, late 17th/early 18th century. Tortoiseshell with silver mounts, the lid with silver and mother-of-pearl inlay. (Any mark would be exceptional.) Bonhams

3. Oblong with cut corners, first quarter 18th century. The style of engraving is typical of the period. Christie's South Kensington

4. Escutcheon shaped, mid-18th century. Many of this type have an inlay of agate in the lid. Sotheby's

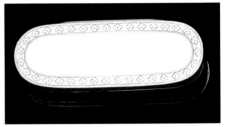

7. Neo-classic oval. The proportions are different from No. 2, not only the oval but also a greater depth of body. Christie's New York

8. Oblong rounded ends, late 18th/early 19th century. Examples of this design are usually quite deep. Christie's New York

9. Oblong engine turned, 19th century. Made in large numbers throughout the 19th century. Christie's New York

10. 'Castle top', mostly second quarter 19th century. In this case Ely Cathedral by Nathaniel Mills II (watch out for new tops). Christie's New York

By the end of the eighteenth century oval (No. 7), eye shaped (No. 6) and canted oblong (oblong with diagonally cut corners) are the principal shapes. From the very early nineteenth century and on the vast majority are oblong (Nos. 9 to 15) or shaped oblong.

Some of the most sought after silver boxes are those with engraved or applied scenes.

131

11. *Hunting scene, 19th century. As with No. 10, watch out for new tops.* Christie's New York

12. *Mid-19th century. The applied floral mounts add to this example, as does the engraved hunting scene (make sure the scene is original). Initials, an armorial or presentation inscription are the norm.* Christie's New York

13. *Shaped oblong, mid-19th century. Usually, as in this case, with a presentation inscription.* Christie's New York

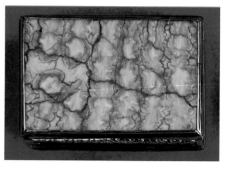

14. *Mammoth tooth, mid-19th century. Although the 19th century preference was for completely silver or gold boxes, examples such as this, made out of exotic materials, may be found.* Bonhams

15. *Pedlar box, 19th century. Much sought after and consequently faked. Notice that this example, which is genuine, is marked on the front (top right-hand corner).* Bonhams

These are usually referred to as 'Castle Tops' (No. 10). See also Vinaigrettes, page 143 and Card Cases, page 137.

Birmingham was a particularly important box making centre in England with Nathaniel Mills being the most sought after maker. London generally produced the finest examples, with John Linnit and Phipps & Robinson being particularly fine and prolific makers.

The second half of the nineteenth century saw a steady decline in production with mostly reproductions being made. Some of these, particularly the gold French and Swiss examples, can be very fine. (Be careful – some have forged marks.)

1. Snuff mull, 18th and 19th century, Scottish. Made out of a ram's horn. The thistles usually indicate a 19th century date. Bonhams

2. Distinctly Scottish form. This snuff mull of the mid-18th century is made of lignum vitae and bone.

SNUFF MULLS

These are a distinctly Scottish form of snuff 'box' found in two types – ram's horn (mid-eighteenth century and nineteenth century examples will often have a cairngorm set in the lid), and oval (mid-eighteenth century and much less common).

The proportions of the oval examples are quite different from the usual oval snuff box. The bulge to the upper part of the body is also a very distinctive feature. Many are made of either silver mounted wood, bone or ivory – a combination of the two will also be found (No. 2), as may all silver examples. The vast majority of both forms, if marked at all, will have a maker's mark only.

During the second half of the nineteenth century complete rams' heads were mounted to make ceremonial snuff mulls (No. 3).

Pitfalls (Snuff Boxes and Mulls)

Damage to hinges is quite common. Make sure that all the knuckles are still properly fixed and that the pin is intact. Hinge repairs are difficult,

expensive and not always very successful. Never force a stiff hinge – put a drop of light oil on it. This is a good idea even if it appears to be working well. Look also for splits in the body at each end of the hinge.

Removal of engravings, re-engraving and covering engraving with a plate are all common problems. If any engraving or applied decoration (e.g. a 'Castle Top') enhances the value significantly then be very certain that it is original to the box.

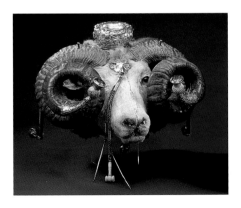

3. Ram's head, late 19th century, Scottish. An actual head mounted on wheels for rolling down the table! Sotheby's

1. Notice the crude engraving on the two early examples (cylinder and tear drop). The classic vase is by Phipps and Robinson – this is one of the most rare and sought after shapes. The canted oblong, top left, is a Birmingham example by Joseph Willmore. Bottom right is a vinaigrette and not a nutmeg grater. Sotheby's

NUTMEG GRATERS

Although never produced at any one time on such a large scale as, say, vinaigrettes, which enjoyed a peak of popularity for some fifty years, nutmeg graters appear to have been produced in fairly steady quantities for the two hundred years from the mid-seventeenth to the mid-nineteenth century.

Nutmeg itself has been known and used in England from medieval times. It was used not only as a spice but also for medicinal purposes, being supposed, for example, to ward off the plague. One possible reason for the appearance of personal graters for nutmeg in the mid-seventeenth century could be the great increase in variety of wines imported into England following the Restoration. Could this discovery of new tastes have stimulated gentlemen to their own variants by the addition of nutmeg?

Whatever the reason for the increased personal use of nutmeg in the second half of the seventeenth century, what did the graters themselves look like? Here we do have a problem since during this period another new vogue was becoming popular – sniffing, or snuffing, grated tobacco. Thus there were also snuff rasps or graters and there are, therefore, two uses to which containers incorporating graters may have been put.

There are two principal types of early graters which could have been for nutmeg, snuff or tobacco. These are the cylindrical examples and the tear drop, heart or pear-shaped graters (No. 1).

The cylindrical examples, which were made up to about the reign of George I, are usually 3in. (7.5cm) long and have a simple pull-off lid at each end. One end, when opened, reveals a small compartment, probably to hold the nutmeg for which it is just the right size. This point favours these graters being used for nutmeg. The other end, when opened, reveals a much longer interior which should have, loose inside it, the cylindrical grater itself. The grater of these examples is normally made of silver and is crudely pierced by literally punching holes through the metal, from what becomes the inside, before the sheet is bent round and soldered to form a tube.

Cylindrical graters of the late seventeenth and early eighteenth centuries are usually rather crudely made and have simple, badly engraved, stylised leaf work on the body and flower heads on the lids (see No. 1). There is a rare octagonal variant of the cylindrical form in the early 18th century.

The heart and tear drop shapes are more rare. They are usually about 1½in. (3.75cm) wide

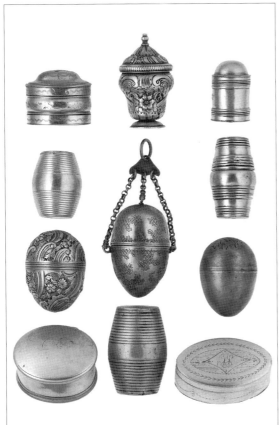

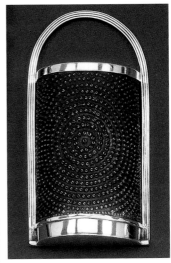

2. (Left) The most unusual of the graters illustrated here is the rococo vase at the top. Quite a bit of variation of proportion can be seen with the barrels, and of decoration with the eggs. The oval boxes date from the late 18th/early 19th century. Notice the shorter cylindrical grater, top right, of the same period.
M. McAleer

3. (Above) Kitchen/butler's grater. Usually dating from the early 19th century. The base is hinged to allow easy removal of the grated nutmeg. Sotheby's

and are decorated similarly to the cylindrical examples. Unlike their contemporary cylindrical graters, the top and bottom lids are hinged, the grater is usually of steel and is fixed into the body.

With both types of early nutmeg grater a marker's mark is all that is usually found.

The middle years of the eighteenth century saw quite an improvement in the quality of workmanship. They also saw new varieties, the most usual being the acorn. This unscrews in the centre to reveal the flat grater which sits on top of the lower section. Of similar construction and period are the egg and the barrel (No. 2). All of these have maker's mark only.

During the late eighteenth century classic vase-shaped (No. 1), oblong, canted oblong (No. 1), circular and oval (No. 2), graters are all

found. There is also a return to a cylindrical form of grater together with a similar type of oval cross section.

With both the vase and the cylindrical forms of this and later periods, a new method of opening is introduced. This is that they open along their length and are hinged at the base. Yet another variant of the cylindrical form has a flap on the side which opens like a door to reveal the grater.

By the late eighteen century graters were properly hallmarked. Some of the finest of this period are the London examples by Phipps and Robinson. The majority, though, were produced by the Birmingham box makers.

A distinctive form known as the kitchen or butler's grater (No. 3) was, it is believed, intended for exactly that – use in the kitchen.

They are usually quite big, 4½in to 5in. (11.5cm to 12.5cm) long, and are clearly not intended to be carried around.

By the mid-nineteenth century few examples were produced and such as are found at or after this period are generally copies of earlier forms.

Pitfalls

The most important pitfalls are with the early cylindrical graters. Since these are usually made of four separate pieces, i.e. body, grater and two lids, any one of these can very easily be replaced. Think also of the possibilities for the unscrupulous if each of the four sections on one original piece has a maker's mark. Four graters, each with one genuine piece with a maker's mark on it, could conceivably be produced! The most common pitfall, though, is the replacement of a missing grater. Always compare the colour of all four pieces; if these are all of the same date they should all have the same colour and patina.

CIGARETTE CASES

Found from the late nineteenth/early twentieth century onwards and produced in very large numbers until the 1960s.

The most common are oblong with rounded corners and sides. Many are also curved so as to fit more comfortably into the pocket.

Concealed spring opening examples (the two halves slide along the length of the hinge to release the lid) are an interesting variation. These enabled you to open the case with one hand.

Engine turned decoration is popular. A small plain oblong cartouche is usually left in one corner for engraved initials, etc.

Amongst the most desirable are enamelled examples. Scenes depicting anything from animals to aircraft are already very collectable. Those depicting naked women are most sought after with erotic scenes commanding the highest prices. (These have always been seriously collected in Germany where most were made.)

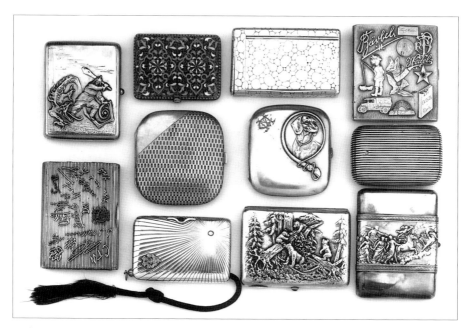

1. From just this small selection it will be seen that the potential for collecting is great. The examples applied with signatures etc. (top right and bottom left) usually result from a presentation.   Christie's South Kensington

2. Always much sought after – the naughtier they are the higher the price. Watch out for fakes.   Bonhams

Pitfalls

Plain examples are now being enamelled with scenes likely to command a good price.

Be wary of stories about examples which saved lives in either the First or Second World War. They are generally fictitious – often an attempt to explain a bad dent which would otherwise ruin the value. I have only ever seen one convincing example. With this the silver had actually been scarred and burnt where the bullet had hit it.

CARD CASES

Although visiting was popular in the eighteenth century and visiting-tickets, as they were known until the end of that century, were extensively used, it is not until the nineteenth century that we find cases being made for them. The earliest literary mention that has so far been found is by Marryat in 1835. Just fifteen years earlier when the Duke of Beaufort's pocket had been picked his visiting cards were mentioned specifically, but nothing is said of a case for them.

Amongst the earliest cases to be found are filigree examples dating from the first quarter of the nineteenth century. Most of these are silver-gilt. Their lids are not often hinged but usually slip over a long bezel. They are unfortunately rarely marked (the only place where they can normally be marked being the solid sides of the bezel). Many filigree examples are Anglo-Indian and are of a much more recent date. They are usually of a shaped outline.

An important characteristic of early examples is the very sharp angles of the corners, a feature that lasts up to the late 1830s and does not reappear in England until the twentieth century.

In the 1830s the first fully marked cases are found. Many have pierced foliate scroll decoration resembling the preceding filigree examples (No. 1).

'Castle Top' cases are today the most sought

1. 'Castle top', early type, simple oblong. This example by Nathaniel Mills II of Birmingham, 1838, has Windsor on one side and Kenilworth on the other. The decoration above and below is pierced (the majority are not). Bonhams

2. 'Castle top' shaped oblong, mid-19th century. Made by Frederick March of Birmingham, this rare scene of St. Anne's Chapel, Edinburgh Castle, at present holds the world record price (£3,600 plus buyer's premium) for a silver card case. Bonhams

after. The term encompasses all scenes, most of which are architectural.

Early examples have scenes on both sides of the case, in a simple rectangle. This contrasts strongly with examples from the 1840s where not only is there normally only one scene, but the foliate scroll decoration follows the outline of the building portrayed (No. 2).

The change to the shaped outline of the sides of the cases took place in the 1840s. 'Castle Tops' continued to be produced until the 1930s, the late examples often having the name of the building incorporated. The views may be either repoussé or engraved.

Engine turning was used throughout the whole period of production.

There is a difference in size between those cases used by men and those used by women. Since the cards used by men were much smaller than those used by women the 'male' card cases are naturally much smaller and are often curved so as to fit more comfortably into a waistcoat pocket.

Engraved rococo decoration dates mostly from after the 1860s and was particularly common around 1900, as was engraved leaf work.

There was a reversion to a more simple, plain oblong outline at the end of the nineteenth century but with rounded corners and slightly bulbous sides making it easy to distinguish from the earlier examples.

During the Edwardian period the idea of fitting a finger ring on a suspensory chain became fashionable. Before this they were normally held in the gloved (white, of course) left hand or occasionally fitted to a chatelaine. The envelope variety, as well as the crocodile skin pattern, were also popular at this time.

Card cases do not seem to have been produced during the First World War. A few were made in the inter-war period. The Second World War finally brought their manufacture to a close.

Unusual examples incorporating stamp holders or with a patented slide for ejecting cards may be found. It is interesting to note that the majority of 'novelty' cases were made for men.

Card cases were not of course made only in England. A good many were produced in the

3. Engraved 'castle top', shaped oblong, mid-19th century. A rare view of Chatsworth House by Nathaniel Mills II, Birmingham 1849. Bonhams

4. Elkington Electrotype. Made by Elkington in both copper, which was then electroplated with silver, and, more rarely, completely in silver. (This example is the former.) Bonhams

Orient for the 'China Trade', Continental examples are met with quite frequently and occasionally an American specimen may be found.

Marking

With the exception of the filigree examples the majority of cases are fully marked, either on the bezel or, less frequently and particularly on early examples, on the base. The lid will normally be partially marked (sometimes on the outside).

The making of silver card cases was completely dominated by Birmingham. Examples marked at other assay offices are rare.

Makers

It is with the earlier cases that the 'names' are to be found, all of whom are from Birmingham. The most sought after is Nathaniel Mills II. Not only was he a fine manufacturer but he was also the most prolific producer of 'Castle Tops'. Others to look for are Joseph Willmore, Edward Smith, George Unite, Taylor & Perry, Yapp & Woodward and W. Dudley.

Condition

As always, of great importance. With card cases look particularly at the hinge which can easily be strained causing slackness and splits. Dents to the sides (especially to cases of shaped outline) are very difficult to remove since there is so little space inside. With repoussé 'Castle Tops' etc. look at the high points where holes may be found through wear. In the case of filigree a close inspection to see that no filigree is missing or damaged is important, these cases being particularly vulnerable.

Fakes

There is at present little or no need to worry about fake card cases since until recently none of them has fetched the sort of price that would normally tempt a forger. Card cases have, however, suffered from the work of forgers who in the past would cut the scenes from 'Castle Top' cases and fit them to the tops of plain snuff boxes, a practice which fortunately is no longer economic.

VESTA BOXES/CASES

In the 1830s a new method of producing a flame was invented, one far easier and more convenient than the tinder box which it rapidly replaced. This invention was a form of wax match named after the Roman goddess Vesta (perhaps because it was so temperamental). The temple of Vesta contained a sacred flame which was tended by the now famous Vestal Virgins.

The heads of these matches were tipped with red phosphorous which would ignite when rubbed against a rough surface. In many cases unfortunate individuals discovered to their discomfort that far less friction was necessary!

In the early years of the vesta people simply adapted existing boxes to contain them, normally by adding a striker to a small silver snuff box. The striker is usually a serrated plate of silver or iron added to the side, base or, on occasions, the interior of the box. As the boxes developed, the strikers were produced by serrating part of the box itself.

Iron strikers, although perhaps the most practical, were quite rare since the laws governing the production of silver forbade the soldering of any base metal to it. There were also the practical problems of soldering these two metals together and, the obvious one of the iron itself rusting. Such strikers, when found, are usually pinned on to the box or on occasions slide into a slot. A useful point when deciding whether an early box is a conversion or not is to look for any decoration continuing behind the striker.

A fascinating and somewhat misunderstood 'extra' found incorporated into some early boxes is a cutter. This is most frequently thought to be for cigars. With nearly all examples, however, the cutter is far too small for such a purpose. Its true function appears to have been for removing the burnt heads of the vestas.

As boxes began to be made specifically for vestas, they quite naturally followed the forms of the snuff boxes from which they had been adapted. But, as in most cases where an existing object has been adapted for a new function, the snuff box form proved not to be entirely satisfactory.

The problem was principally the way in which the lid opened, exposing the vestas to the greatest extent. This markedly increased the risk of a stray spark entering the box, setting off what was little short of a small incendiary bomb.

The answer was simple – the lid was moved to the end of the box. It could then hold as many vestas and, at the same time, a far smaller area would be exposed on opening. The earliest so far discovered of this form dates from 1845 and was made by Nathaniel Mills II.

To hold the lid firmly closed an interior spring was added. This would stop any accidental opening of the box in one's pocket. It is important when examining any vesta box to ensure that this spring is still in place and intact, for its loss or damage will detract from the box. Should there be none evident, examine the interior for a slot at the base where one was originally fitted. Look also for a peg next to the hinge against which the spring acted.

The interiors were nearly always gilded to prevent the chemicals of the vesta heads from reacting with the silver.

With the important changes which we have seen above, the vesta box from this period on developed quite independently of contemporary snuff boxes.

One of the earliest and most noticeable independent developments was the rounding off of the sharp corners and edges which would cause rapid wear inside a waistcoat pocket.

Boxes are quite frequently found to which suspensory rings have been fixed. These appear to have been added at the whim of individual customers for attachment to chatelaines or alberts, and could perhaps be regarded as an optional extra.

The size of the vast majority of surviving examples is between 1½in. and 2¼in. (3.8 and 5.7cm) long. This size was dictated by the vestas themselves, which were rather smaller than modern matches. Any boxes found outside this range are unusual and are generally of the novelty type. The smallest silver vesta box so far recorded is an example 1in. (2.5cm) long.

1. Although most are of the standard shape, these are, almost without exception, all enhanced by their decoration. The enamels of naked ladies are (as with cigarette cases) the most valuable. Sotheby's

2. Sentry box. A series of these, each enamelled with a soldier from a different regiment, was produced in the late 19th century (the design was registered in 1885.). They are today amongst the most valuable of all vestas.   Sotheby's

The independence of the vesta developed to the extent that the positioning of the hallmarks was changed. Snuff boxes had usually been struck with a full set of marks on the interior of the base and a partial set inside the lid. With the true vesta box a full set will normally be struck

on the bezel (the strip of metal over which the lid fits) and a partial set in the lid.

The snuff box form made predominantly in the early years will nearly always be found bearing London hallmarks. It should be noted that throughout the history of these boxes the finest examples of workmanship were nearly always made in this centre. This applied even after the capital had lost its dominance in their production, examples struck with London marks after 1890 being quite rare.

Birmingham was the centre which took over from London, the bulk of boxes being made there from about 1890 until the vesta box itself ceased to be produced after the First World War.

A good many boxes from the 1890s and early 1900s will be found bearing Chester hallmarks. The vast majority of these will have been made in Birmingham.

Boxes which bear the marks of any of the other assay offices still operating in the nineteenth century are quite rare, and thus sought after. The offices involved are Sheffield, Exeter, York, Newcastle, Edinburgh, Glasgow, and Dublin. Of these Sheffield is the most frequently encountered.

The end for the vesta box came with the First World War and the introduction of the petrol lighter. This was first used by French soldiers and naturally spread rapidly through the trenches.

As the vesta box started as a modification of the snuff box, so in turn the petrol lighter was a modification of the vesta box. Even today the form of the vesta box is immediately apparent in most pocket lighters.

It is interesting to note, while mentioning lighters, that a form of vesta box was produced in the 1860s which incorporated a wick. This could be used when a more permanent flame was required.

Broadly speaking, boxes may be grouped under three major categories. First, the snuff box form, produced mostly in the formative years of these boxes in London. Secondly, the true vesta box, or case, as it may be described, nearly all of which were made in Birmingham. Thirdly and last, the novelty type, under which examples performing more than one function and trick opening boxes may also be grouped.

With all three major groups, variations in type of decoration are fairly universal, plain, engraved, chased, gilt and enamelled being found with each.

The snuff box form sometimes has its lid enamelled with a representation of the visiting card of the original owner. The incorporation of a cutter is also an important variation found with this group. Apart from the conventional oblong, examples are round, square, peardrop, heart, shield, or kidney shaped.

At the end of the nineteenth and beginning of the twentieth century a good many advertising examples will be found. Advertising boxes are mostly of base metal and were given away with various products.

Novelty boxes are amongst the most interesting. The earliest are the trick opening examples of snuff box form. From the late nineteenth century on many other novelties were produced, the most common being the animals and musical instruments which were mostly made in base metal. A good many in the shape of books were produced. These were often in vulcanite and decorated with the busts of such people as Edward VII. Amongst the more unusual novelty boxes are the sporran, the dog and the dog kennel, the head, the cigars, the baby, the sentry box, the snake and, perhaps most amusing of all, the corseted bust of a woman.

Under the novelty grouping may also be placed the combination of function boxes. The most usual are those which combine a sovereign or stamp holder. Whistles and penknives may be found, although more rare, as also are perpetual calendars and compasses.

Pictorial boxes are to be found in all three groups and are now highly sought after. The finest are usually the enamelled examples although good chased, stamped and engraved specimens may be found.

Collectors have little to worry about in the way of fakes. Until recently few people have shown much interest in these boxes and prices have therefore been far too low to attract the interest of the unscrupulous.

It is still possible to purchase interesting examples at reasonable prices. New types are still being discovered, so there is plenty of scope for the new collector.

VINAIGRETTES

The vinaigrette presents great and varied opportunities to the collector for, although its effective period of production is short, from about 1780 to the mid-nineteenth century a seemingly infinite variety was produced.

The principal feature which distinguishes the vinaigrette from any other form of small box, is the grille. This is usually revealed on opening the lid and will normally appear as a second hinged and pierced 'lid'. The function of this is to hold a sponge in place and at the same time to allow the aromatic substance with which the sponge inside is soaked to filter through.

With early vinaigrettes, i.e. eighteenth century and very early nineteenth century examples, the piercing of the grille will usually be quite simple geometric patterns. As the nineteenth century progressed the piercing of the grilles became more elaborate and was normally combined with engraving. The most usual design was foliate scrolls.

1. Book form, 19th century. This is interesting in itself but is made even more collectable by virtue of its grille which has musical decoration. Sotheby's

2. A selection of some of the types available. The Maltese cross is particularly difficult to find.

Sotheby's

Should a vinaigrette be found with a grille other than the geometric or foliate scroll designs mentioned above then this will enhance its value. Among the variants that may be found are military trophies, musical instruments, filigree work, tartans, birds, books and quills, Prince of Wales plumes and, perhaps the most famous of all, the grille of the Nelson commemorative vinaigrette which depicts the *Victory.*

The grille of a vinaigrette should always be gilded. This was done to prevent the aromatic substance within from reacting with the silver. For the same reason the whole of the interior should be gilded.

The condition and originality of the grille is obviously of great importance. A replaced or damaged grille will have a considerable effect on the value of any vinaigrette. Almost invariably the grille will be hinged on the right-hand side when the vinaigrette is opened. Any exception to this should be very carefully examined for signs of replacement or even conversion from small snuff box to vinaigrette.

Most damage to grilles has been caused by people forcing stiff hinges and ultimately breaking them off. Never force a stiff hinge – with a drop of fine oil and a bit of patience you should easily cure the problem.

If grilles had been regularly marked it would have been very useful in determining their originality. Unfortunately this was not the case and even when a marked grille is found the marks are often partially cut away by the piercing which was done after the hallmarking.

Great care should be taken with any unusual grille since unscrupulous individuals have 'improved' examples by changing the grilles.

The actual shapes and decorations of vinaigrettes vary enormously.

Early examples, those of the eighteenth and early nineteenth century, are of simple outline. This will most often be a canted oblong, oblong with rounded corners or, less frequently, oval. The decoration during this period is simple, most usually engraved and/or bright cut engraved, geometric patterns and stylised flower heads. A good many around the turn of the century are quite plain on the outside.

From the early nineteenth century and for the rest of the period of production of vinaigrettes, engine turning was very popular, a great variety of geometric patterns being produced.

By the 1830s borders of foliate scroll and floral decoration are found. The idea for this probably developed from the increasing elaboration of the thumb pieces on boxes in the 1820s.

By the 1840s most vinaigrettes are of shaped oblong or shaped oval form.

The value of any vinaigrette of conventional box form varies greatly depending on the nature of decoration. The most common forms are the engraved geometric patterns and engine turning discussed above together with foliate scroll and floral engraving.

3. Second half 19th century combined vinaigrette (perfume bottle) of cornucopia form.

Private Collection

Particularly sought after are the pictorial vinaigrettes referred to as 'Castle Tops' (although only a few actually depict castles). These may be divided into two groups, repoussé tops and engraved tops. Of these two groups, scene for scene, the repoussé tops are the most valuable. It should be remembered that the comparative rarity of the different scenes has quite an effect on value.

So far vinaigrettes of conventional box type have been discussed, but a large number of novelty vinaigrettes were also produced and these, with the pictorial boxes, form the most valuable group.

The earliest of these novelty examples are the eggs, closely followed by books, purses, watches, fish and the famous Nelson Memorial vinaigrette.

As the nineteenth century progressed more and more novelty forms were produced, amongst these the Maltese Cross, shells, cornucopias, crowns, animal heads, lamps, leaves, nuts, cane tops, thistles, sporrans, barrels, baskets of flowers, and acorns.

The Victorian carnation vinaigrette is one of the most delightful (No. 4). This is pierced in such a way as to allow the perfume to permeate through the petals.

One of the most sought after examples is the recumbent cow. Great care must be taken before acquiring one. I have examined a number and have not found a genuine example yet. All had been converted from butter tub finials of the nineteenth century and were marked on the body of the cow only.

4. Carnation, a rare mid-19th century form. The perfume is released through the petals.   M. McAleer

During the middle years of the nineteenth century combined vinaigrettes and perfume bottles were produced (No. 5). The three most usual forms are the single scent bottle with vinaigrette base, the double scent bottle with central vinaigrette, and the cornucopia.

With improvements in personal hygiene and drainage towards the end of the nineteenth century the necessity for vinaigrettes ceased.

Examples by such makers as Nathaniel Mills of Birmingham and Sampson Mordan of London always command a premium, the former being most famous for his 'Castle Tops' and the latter for novelty vinaigrettes.

Pitfalls

Those mentioned when discussing grilles (see above).

Condition, as always.

Re-engraved tops are a great danger. Always examine any engraved scene for signs of the removal of previous engraving.

With repoussé tops always ensure that the top is original.

Be suspicious of recumbent cows! I have yet to be shown a genuine example (see above).

5. Mid-19th century combined vinaigrettes and perfume bottles. Left: double perfume with central vinaigrette. Right: single perfume with vinaigrette base.   Private Collection

CHAPTER 13

Small Collectables

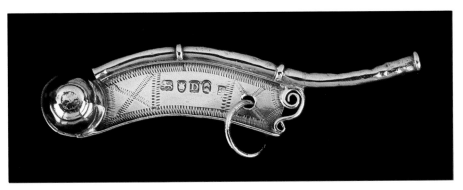

1. Standard form, late 18th century. London 1799 by Peter and Ann Bateman.   Christie's New York

BOATSWAINS' CALLS

The boatswain's call was, and still is, used on ships to give orders, the high pitched note being able to be heard through the roar of the sea. It is because of this old system of giving commands that whistling became an offence on board ship.

Silver examples can be found dating back to the mid-eighteenth century. For the romantically inclined these early calls present a fascinating field for collecting, there being every possibility that they were used at such battles as the Nile, Copenhagen or even Trafalgar. The value of any call is considerably increased when there is positive evidence to connect it with such important events.

There are three parts to boatswains' calls. The barrel or boy, the pipe or cannon, and the keel. To the keel a suspensory ring will be fitted. Most of the earlier (mid-eighteenth century calls to be found are rather crude and were probably made from melted coins by the ship's coppersmith or tinsmith. By the end of the eighteenth century most calls were produced by silversmiths and are of a much

better quality, although lacking some of the charm of the earlier ones.

A useful guide to date is to look at the ends of the barrel. This should be decorated with an anchor. On early examples this will normally be crudely hand chased. Later eighteenth century and early nineteenth century calls will have finely chased or engraved anchors. By the mid-nineteenth century they generally have die stamped anchors. Twentieth century calls are normally mass-produced electro-plate or base metal. These will be stamped with a crude arrow rather than an anchor.

Examples of the mid-eighteenth century are rarely marked, but from the late eighteenth century onwards silver calls are usually fully hallmarked. A famous silversmith, such as Paul Storr, will considerably enhance the value. Engraved names of ships, naval bases or individuals will also add considerably to value.

Pitfalls

The saline atmosphere in which calls were used was highly corrosive and parts sometimes

2. Standard form, early 19th century.

M. McAleer

had to be replaced.

As mentioned above, examples engraved with some form of identification are much more valuable. Beware, therefore, ordinary calls which have had such identification added by unscrupulous individuals.

MENU/PLACE CARD HOLDERS

Popular for a short period in the late nineteenth/early twentieth century, these have become increasingly collected. Individual examples may be found, although a good many remain in sets. If cased this is a plus factor.

The most sought after have enamel plaques (usually discs) decorated with sporting motifs – pheasants, hares, game dogs, etc. (No. 1)

Pitfalls

New interesting/rare enamel could, as with cigarette cases, be a danger.

1. Cased set with enamels depicting game birds.

Christie's South Kensington

2. Owls are always sought after items.

Christie's South Kensington

PINCUSHIONS

Two basic groups may be found – dressing table and 'portable'.

Dressing table examples may be divided between those forming part of a toilet service and individual, often novelty, examples.

It is reasonable to assume that any large – usually about 6in. (15cm) wide – oblong example dating from the seventeenth or eighteenth centuries will have been part of a toilet service (No. 1). In some cases the pincushion will be set on the lid of a casket. The filling, if original, usually contains an abrasive powder to keep the pins clean. This was because the steel that the pins were made from would rust very easily.

The most collectable today are the individual novelty examples. These mostly date from the late nineteenth/early twentieth centuries. A great variety of creatures are to be found. Pigs, chicks and elephants are quite common (unless of unusual size) whereas fish, goats and lizards are all rare types.

Objects may also be found, with shoes the most common. Most others, such as wheelbarrows, are scarce, whereas a roller skate (No. 2) is rare.

Small portable examples usually have a

1. A William III pincushion. Part of a toilet service by John Readshaw made in London in 1697.

Sotheby's

suspensory ring for attachment to a chatelaine. Usually these have stuffing held behind velvet between two plates, often discs, of silver. The pins are then pushed into the edge or side of the 'cushion'.

Pitfalls

Condition is often a problem with novelty examples, most of which were quite cheaply made from thin sheet silver.

If buying a rare example make certain that it is in period (reproductions are common) and is genuine.

2. Novelty pincushions of the late 19th/early 20th century. The roller skate is particularly rare.
Christie's South Kensington

1. A selection of late 17th/early 18th century toy/miniature silver.   Christie's New York

TOYS AND MINIATURES

Examples may be found from the seventeenth century onwards, with the Dutch the most prolific makers. Apart from all the objects usually made in silver, virtually anything else may also turn up from bureaux to villages – nothing would surprise me.

With the more conventional objects – teapots, candlesticks, etc. – a popular idea is that they were travellers' samples or apprentice pieces. This is not the case. There were specialist makers; David Clayton is a good example, dominating, as he did, production in early eighteenth century London. George Manjoy had done much the same in the late seventeenth century.

Examples from the seventeenth century may be found with full marking. Most, however, if marked at all, have the maker's mark only.

WINE FUNNELS

Mostly produced in the last quarter of the eighteenth and first half of the nineteenth century.

Early examples are simple funnels. By the 1770s/'80s they are made in two sections – the bowl, which is pierced so as to remove cork, large lumps of sediment, etc., and the narrow funnel section. A piece of muslin was fixed (usually with a ring) below the bowl to remove any fine sediment. The end of the funnel was always curved to direct the flow to the side of the decanter.

An alternative construction has the pierced strainer section fitting inside the complete funnel.

By 1800 ribs are found where the funnel sits in the top of the decanter. These allow air to escape, giving a smoother flow.

The so-called 'thumbpiece' on the top edge was for clipping the funnel on to the edge of a punch bowl.

Some may be found with stands.

Pitfalls

A missing ring is not a problem – most people do not realise that there should be one. It is quite often there but so jammed up with polish etc. that its existence isn't even noticed.

The end of the funnel is unacceptable if split. Rather than being properly repaired many have been trimmed. The result is that the end loses all or part of its curve – such examples should be avoided.

WINE LABELS

With the increased variety of wines in use following the Restoration and, subsequently, the evolution of the practice of decanting wine into glass, there was a need for a method of labelling. The wine label was the result.

During the eighteenth century the name wine label was not used. They were known instead as bottle tickets although by the end of the eighteenth century the name bottle label was applied.

The earliest labels (1730/60) are nearly all of the escutcheon type but some of rococo form

1. Early 19th century with its stand. Notice the shell 'thumbpiece' and the ribs. Sotheby's

with bacchanalian decoration of this period are known.

Many of the early labels are by a man with perhaps the most improbable name for a maker of wine labels, Sandilands Drinkwater. A close neighbour of Sandilands Drinkwater and another early maker was John Harvey.

By the 1750s bottle tickets were well established although it is not until the 1770s that they are found in large numbers.

There are four groups into which labels may initially be divided: first those suspended by chains round the neck of a bottle or decanter; secondly those which are held by means of a ring round the neck of a bottle or decanter; thirdly complete rings, and fourthly those which are fixed on to the top of a cork or stopper. Of these four groups the vast majority of labels fit into the first.

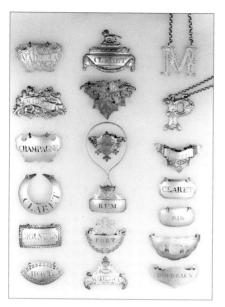

1. (Above, left) Notice particularly the labels in the first vertical row which, with the exception of the Hock label, are all by Sandilands Drinkwater, the escutcheons being the most common. In the second vertical row the heraldic Claret label of the Regency period is a great rarity, whereas the heraldic Madeira label at the bottom with its engraved cartouche is more common. The Rum label with a wire neck-ring is uncommon. In the third row the initials are Scottish, the others are all foreign.   Sotheby's

2. (Above, right) A selection of plain, rounded and canted oblongs together with an oval. These all have common titles. Notice the smaller sauce label for Ketchup in the centre.   M. McAleer

3. (Left) Of particular interest are the fine pierced labels. Notice that part of the piercing has been damaged on the Port label; this will detract from its value. Rarities are the Vidonia, the Cyder and the Maltese cross shaped Sherry label.
                                     Sotheby's

5. These nearly all show interesting variations from the more usual forms. Particular rarities are the Hollands decorated with fruit above, grapes and vines below, the star-shaped Port, and the Sherry with the Prince of Wales plumes above.   Sotheby's

4. A group of seemingly ordinary labels whose interest and value lie in their nearly all being from provincial assay offices. Notice the extremely rare title Deides Helmer, also the crescent-shaped Old Sheffield plate label with an aperture for the addition of a title decorated with a seated gourmand.   Sotheby's

Beyond this one may divide labels by method of manufacture, by method of displaying the title, by whether gilded or not, by styles, by titles and by makers.

Let us examine each of these and see just how specialised one may become when collecting bottle tickets.

First, the methods by which these labels were made. Most labels were produced from sheet silver which, as in the case of the early escutcheons, would be cut to the desired shape and could then be decorated by engraving or chasing.

With the development of more industrialised methods in the late eighteenth century many labels were die stamped from sheet silver. This applies particularly to many Regency and Victorian examples such as the vine leaves

6. Of particular interest are the two classic urn-shaped labels (Mountain and Brandy). Of the two the shape of the Brandy label is the rarer. The Madeira label above this with its pierced border is very unusual.   Sotheby's

7. (Above) A fine example of the leopard's pelt label by Paul Storr together with a rare pair of Bacchanalian mask labels by Digby Scott and Benjamin Smith. The two letters are from Birmingham (most individual letters are Scots). Sotheby's

8. (Left) A good selection of grape and vine labels, in particular the unusual Brandy label surmounted by a winged female bust. The urn-shaped Red Port is a rarity – it was made c.1800 by Phipps and Robinson. Sotheby's

and the bacchanalian labels.

The finest labels were always made by the process of casting. These will always be thicker and heavier than similar labels of sheet silver. The backs of such labels generally have a rather rough surface from the casting.

Following naturally from the methods by which the labels themselves were produced are the ways by which the titles themselves were displayed.

These may either be engraved, engraved and filled, pierced, cast with the body of the label or made separately and slotted into the back of the label. Of the five methods listed above the last two methods are quite rare.

Yet another distinction may be made between gilded and plain white silver labels. By far the greater number of labels will be of plain white silver, most gilded examples being from the Regency period by such makers as Paul Storr, Digby Scott and Benjamin Smith.

The styles of labels follow naturally the prevailing style of the period of production.

Mid–eighteenth century labels are usually of the escutcheon form or on rare occasions a scroll with grapes, vines and bacchanals. With the development of neo-classicism in the second half of the eighteenth century labels formed as crescents, classic urns and scrolls were produced together with oblongs, canted oblongs and ovals, the last three being the most common forms of all and produced in large numbers into the nineteenth century.

The Regency saw the production of some quite massive labels of grape and vine form, together with the famous leopard's pelts of Paul Storr (derived from the Warwick vase) and various rococo revival bacchanal labels. During the late Regency and Victorian period vine leaves, sometimes with grapes, predominate.

By the mid-nineteenth century the bottle ticket was declining in popularity because a new law required vintners to stick labels on to their bottles.

Other forms that should be mentioned are pierced borders (mostly late eighteenth century), escallop shells (early nineteenth century), initials and titles – where the title itself is cut out to produce the label – (both nineteenth century),

Great rarities are the Star of the late eighteenth century, the Bat, and, the Four Leaf Clover of the Regency and the Free Trade labels of about 1860.

Amongst the most sought after of all labels are heraldic examples. Theses are either (A) formed completely as a family crest, (B) surmounted by a crest or (C) engraved with one. With heraldic labels it must be remembered that only one set would normally have been produced for a family and, unless the set was of any size, each label would be unique for its particular title.

Apart from the style of a label the greatest single factor that will affect its value is its title. The more obscure this is the more valuable will be the label. Thus Port, Claret, Madeira, Lisbon, Sherry, Bordeaux, Brandy, Hock and Gin are all common, whereas Champagne, Teneriffe and Whisky (eighteenth century) are quite scarce and titles such as St Georges, Est-Est, Frontiniac and Old Tom are rarities. In all, over one thousand names and variants have been recorded so that if you wish to collect examples of each title a lifetime's work lies before you.

The maker of a particular bottle ticket is naturally of importance, some collections being based on the work of an individual silversmith. The most interesting are perhaps Sandilands Drinkwater, John Harvey, Susannah Barker, Hester Bateman, Phipps and Robinson, Scott and Smith, Paul Storr, Benjamin and James Smith, and Rawlings and Summers.

Pitfalls

Cast fakes which use an original label as a pattern.

New titles. Always examine every title very carefully for signs of an earlier one. This applies particularly to rare titles.

CHAPTER 14

Silver Plate

An ability to distinguish between the various plating techniques is important. Although the subject may appear rather daunting at first, once you know a few ground rules you should not have too much trouble.

There are, however, no short cuts. The best way to real understanding is to know how the different types of plating were carried out. Armed with this knowledge the 'ground rules' should make sense.

Four basic methods of plating concern us: Close Plating, French Plating, Old Sheffield or Fused Plating and Electroplating. (Of these French Plating could almost be eliminated, being so rarely encountered).

CLOSE PLATING

Although a very ancient method you are unlikely to encounter any examples made before the end of the eighteenth century.

Close plating was, until the second half of the nineteenth century, the only way in which it was possible to cover iron or steel with silver. Since the metals have no affinity with each other it is not possible to stick silver directly on to iron or steel. To get round this problem tin was used as a 'glue'.

To make a piece of close plate the object was first made in steel. The surfaces were then prepared (they had to be grit, grease, moisture, and blemish free) and coated with flux (sal ammoniac was used). The object was then heated and covered in molten tin. Whilst the tin was still molten prepared foils of silver (rather like but a bit thicker than kitchen foil) were laid on the surface and smoothed out.

The great advantage of using this technique was that it enabled an object to be made with a good cutting edge which at the same time looked like silver. (It is impossible to produce a good cutting edge using only silver or copper.)

It is hardly surprising that the objects most often found are knives and forks (usually sets of dessert or fish eaters with mother-of-pearl, ivory etc. handles), candle snuffers, grape shears, skewers, scissors and some flatware. Soup ladles are the largest item likely to be encountered.

Marks

Most close plate is marked. Characteristically the marks will usually give the visual impression of a set of hallmarks. An unusual feature of the marking is that the maker's name (e.g. Gilbert, Prime or Harwood) is given in full and is split with one 'half' above the other.

These makers' name punches will be struck most often with geometric (rather like alchemy symbols) punches, usually repeated a couple of times.

Gilbert is the most commonly encountered maker. Some confusion has arisen with some of his marks because of his use of the letters P.S. in a punch closely resembling that of Paul Storr (see No. 2). The letters actually stand for Plated Steel, however much some may try to imply an involvement with Storr!

If there are no marks on a piece how can you tell if it is close plated?

Try sticking a magnet to the piece. If it does not stick then it cannot be; if it does then there are only two possibilities: close plate or electroplate on steel (see page 165).

Look at any sharp edges or corners where wear is most likely to have occurred. With close plate these show as dark grey (black edges).

Pitfalls

Any damage is virtually impossible to repair and re-plating is difficult and usually unsuccessful. (There is no one today able to close plate so only the electroplating technique can be used.)

Avoid pieces with 'blisters' – these result from either the steel body rusting or the tin spontaneously changing its form. Both are serious problems.

FRENCH PLATE

Only rarely encountered. Pieces when found usually date from the late seventeenth century through to the mid-eighteenth century.

The piece was made first from brass. After surface preparation (as with close plate) the heated object had leaf silver burnished on to its surface. A large range of objects was produced, from candlesticks and casters to salvers and soup tureens.

Although many pieces survive today that would originally have been French plate they cannot in most cases be identified as such, all the silver having long since been polished from the surface. As a result they are today in collections not as French plate but as fine examples of late seventeenth/early eighteenth century brass. Always look for traces of silver in 'awkward to polish' nooks and crannies on any fine pieces of brass of this period.

OLD SHEFFIELD PLATE
(FUSED PLATE)

First produced in about 1743 by Thomas Boulsover, a cutler of Sheffield, and unquestionably the finest form of plating ever produced.

Unlike all other forms of plating, where the object was made first and then covered with silver, with Old Sheffield plating the object was made out of the already plated metal.

It is this that led to nearly all the major differences between Old Sheffield and other

forms of plating and is fundamental to an understanding of it.

Producing the plated metal from which the object was made required a considerable amount of work.

First a specially alloyed (it contained zinc and lead) ingot of copper had a sheet of sterling standard silver placed on top of it. This sheet would be slightly smaller than the top of the ingot. A plate of steel was placed on top of this to protect the surface of the silver from the blows with a sledge hammer which followed. Known as 'bedding in' this ensured as perfect a contact as possible between the silver and the copper ingot.

Having done this and removed the steel sheet, the top was covered with a layer of chalk to prevent the copper sheet which was next placed on the top from adhering to the silver when molten. (The reason for the copper sheet was to prevent oxygen from being absorbed by the silver when molten.)

Binding wires were then put around and this extraordinary sandwich was placed in a furnace. The ingot was carefully watched in the furnace. A trickle of silver running down the side of the ingot (this was known as the ingot 'weeping') indicated that the silver was molten. Once removed, cooled down, tidied and cleaned, the ingot (now a block of copper with silver fused to its top) could be reduced to sheet fused plate of the required thickness from which objects could then be made.

It is quite extraordinary how much work and skill was required just to get to this stage and produce a sheet of copper with a layer of silver fused to one side (known as single plate).

Even more complex was the plating of both sides (double plate), first produced in 1763 and well established by 1770. If 'double plate' seems daunting then imagine trying to produce wire – this they achieved by 1768.

Like many inventors, Boulsover did not realise the true commercial potential of his discovery; all that he seems to have produced were buttons and snuff boxes. The man who realised the potential and developed Boulsover's invention was Joseph Hancock of Sheffield, who from the mid-1750s started to make a much wider range of objects such as saucepans, candlesticks and coffee pots. It was probably a pair of Hancock's candlesticks that Horace Walpole purchased in 1760 for two guineas, which he described as being quite pretty.

Just how Hancock obtained the secret of Old Sheffield plate is unknown. It is often said, but with no supporting evidence, that he was one of Boulsover's apprentices. The apprentice records of this period give two Joseph Hancocks, neither of them apprentice to Boulsover, but significantly one of them apprenticed to one of his relations. Both Boulsover and Hancock, eventually gave up making objects and specialised in producing sheets of fused plate, which were retailed to other manufacturers.

Other early manufacturers were Nathaniel Smith c.1756, Thomas Law c.1758, and Tudor and Leader who established the first true factory for producing fused plate objects in about 1760. It is this year that can reasonably be taken as the start of large scale production.

Having examined the background, just how is it possible to know with certainty when you have a piece of 'Old Sheffield'?

With experience it is possible to recognise pieces stylistically, the same patterns appearing quite frequently. This results from the process being essentially an industrialised one. More positive methods than this are of course necessary.

First, and most obviously, establish what the base metal is. If copper, then the object may or may not be Old Sheffield plate. If anything other than copper, it is safest to dismiss any idea of it being Old Sheffield. (There are exceptions in the 1840s.) It is a useful point that the colour of the copper of Old Sheffield is normally rather brown, due to the alloying of zinc and lead discussed above. With electroplate the copper is usually distinctly red, since there is no need for alloys to be used. When copper shows with Old Sheffield, the object is said to be bleeding.

Having established that the object has copper as its base metal, depending on the construction of the object the seams should next be looked for. These are of great

3. Seam on beaker, c.1800.

importance, since the appearance of these will be able to tell you if the object is fused plate or not. Solder joins or seams will show as 'yellow' stains on the silver with fused plate (No. 3), whereas with electroplate they will be covered with silver. It is important to remember that, regardless of the form of plating, a solder line will always show where the silver has been worn off and that a bad solder join will show as a line under electroplate, but with no 'yellow' stain. It should also be borne in mind that when Old Sheffield plate has been electroplated, the solder lines will be covered.

In itself the presence of a good seam should be sufficient, but since not all objects have these, other features must also be looked for.

Objects such as teapots, coffee pots, tankards and urns were usually constructed of single plate having their copper interiors tinned to prevent verdigris from poisoning the users.

This tinning was done by first covering all the silver surfaces of the vessel with shellac to protect them. Molten tin was then poured inside, swirled around and the excess poured

4. Snuffers tray, c.1760/5, made using two sheets of fused plate.

out. Tinning will also frequently be found on the bottoms of trays and salvers, and on the insides of wine coolers. The colour of the tin will vary from a light polished silver/grey inside tankards to a dark grey/green under salvers and trays. The presence of tinning on an object indicates that it is Old Sheffield (copper cooking utensils were also tinned), and certainly rules out any possibility of it being electroplate.

Until the development of double plate, manufacturers were presented with the problem of how to make such things as the lids of tankards with silver on two surfaces where the underside would show when in use. This was overcome by making two lids, one with silver on the upper, and the other with silver on the lower surface, fitting these together and lapping the edge of the top one (made deliberately larger) over, thus holding the two firmly together.

The same technique was employed for a different reason in the construction of early salvers and snuffers trays (No. 4). Here the problem was not that the lower surface would show, which it obviously would not, but that of producing a strong salver with sharp die-stamped edges. If the salver or tray was to be made of a single sheet of fused plate, and be strong enough for use, this sheet would be too thick for a good sharp die stamping to be produced. On the other hand if a sheet thin enough to produce a good die stamping was used, it would be too weak for use. Two stampings were therefore made and joined together, one from thin fused plate for the top

to give sharp edge decoration, and the other from thick plate for the bottom to give strength. With the development of separate die-stamped and applied edges in the late 1780s (see below), this technique died out.

Casting, or rather lack of it, is of great importance when establishing if a piece is Old Sheffield plate or not. It must always be remembered that it was impossible to cast fused plate. Therefore, all the parts which on an object made of silver or electroplate would be cast, e.g. spouts, finials and handle sockets of coffee pots, have in the case of fused plate to be constructed from die-stamped sections of sheet metal (No. 5). The easiest way of distinguishing between the cast and the die-stamped part is to examine the seam. First for solder 'stain' (see above) and secondly, in the case of handles, for any slight gaps which indicate a hollow die-stamped part rather than a solid cast section. Also with castings, metal will frequently stand proud of the surface at this point where the 'flash' has not been properly removed. A granular appearance (No. 7) also indicates casting.

Piercing presented no real difficulty after the introduction of double plating and was done by fly punching (a mechanical form of piercing). It would be thought that piercing would expose raw copper, but this is not the case since as the punch cut through the fused plate it dragged silver through with it, automatically covering most of the exposed copper. Hand piercing was done on rare occasions and such pieces will show copper in the piercing.

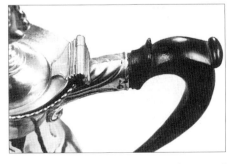

5. Handle socket constructed from two die-stamped halves.

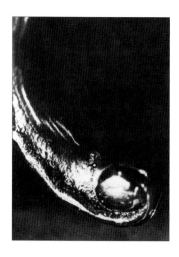

6 (Above). Teapot, c.1780, the engraved initials cut through to copper.

7 (Left). Granular surface on a cast handle.

Engraving (No. 6) presented great difficulties for once copper was exposed by an engraving there was no way in which it could be concealed. To avoid this foliate scrollwork, classic festoons and bright-cutting were normally achieved by flat chasing (No. 8). It is quite straightforward to see when this has been done, since a ghost impression of the decoration will be seen on the reverse side. This should never be present when the decoration has been engraved.

Flat chasing could not produce sufficiently sharp or fine lines to give a satisfactory impression of an engraved coat-of-arms, crest or initials. These therefore continued to be properly engraved. Thus the engraving of these will often be seen to cut through the skin of silver, exposing copper (No. 6). A more heavily plated sheet was sometimes used on a section where it was anticipated that an engraving would be executed.

In about 1790 the idea of 'letting-in' shields of either fused plate with an extra thick layer of silver, or on rare occasions silver itself, was developed. With objects bearing let-in shields the area to be engraved was cut out and the 'shield' soldered into its place. Evidence of the solder line will usually be seen on the reverse side, even when tinned.

Let-in sections were not confined simply to armorials and initials, but will be found used extensively for bands of bright-cut decoration.

A cheaper method of achieving the same ends was employed from about 1810 onwards. This was to rub-in a thin sheet of pure silver with the use of heat and the pressure of a burnisher.

8. Underside of snuffers tray, c.1820, showing a ghost impression of the decoration as a result of flat-chasing.

9. Entrée dish, c.1810, with rubbed-in silver shield.

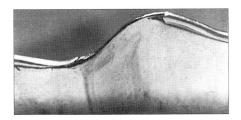

10. Damaged plain silver wire edge.

Rubbed-in shields are the ones most usually found and are most visible when the objects bearing them are tarnished since being of pure silver they take much longer to discolour even slightly (No. 9). If either a rubbed-in or a let-in shield is present the object will be fused plate.

The introduction by Roberts and Cadman of silver edges in about 1785 was a major improvement. Edges had long been a problem and the raw copper edge itself had normally been concealed by burnishing it over and tinning it. There still remained, however, an edge of fused plate which received the hardest treatment during polishing and was usually the first part to bleed. Their idea was to solder on and burnish over a thin plain strip of silver thus protecting this vulnerable area (No. 10). Soon beaded (1780s), reeded (1790s), and gadrooned (1800s) silver wire edges were being produced. Eventually the idea went far beyond the production of simple wires and ended in elaborate foliate scroll, floral, and shell silver edge mounts being produced. These could not be rolled as wire, but had to be individually stamped in steel dies from thin sheets of silver. Mounts of this type had to be filled with lead to give them strength, otherwise ordinary finger pressure would be sufficient to crush them.

The presence of silver edges and mounts is reasonably straightforward to detect. Plain edging will normally stand proud of the surface and can easily be both seen and felt. More elaborate edging (e.g. gadrooning), will naturally stand proud of the main surface, but will be burnished over underneath where it can again be both felt and seen easily, especially when the under surface has been tinned.

With late pieces (1830s), burnishing over does not often appear, but there are fortunately other indications of these mounts. Bleeding on less exposed parts but not on the edges is a good guide. A dull grey colour (the exposed lead filling) on the high points of the mounts will also indicate a lead filled mount. Naturally these indications do not apply to pieces in pristine condition. Since silver mounts and edges are normally only found on fused plate, their presence on an object is a reasonably good, though not infallible, guide that the object is Old Sheffield plate.

Even at the height of the Regency period when contemporary silver was extensively gilded, gilding will only rarely be found on Old Sheffield plate. It will normally be found only on the interiors of objects such as cream jugs and salts where it was very necessary. The reason for this lack of gilding was that the mercurial or fire gilding process had to be used (see page 37).

It was the degree of heat involved during the fire gilding which was the problem with Old Sheffield plate. This was sufficient to melt any lead or soft solder, thus making it impossible to gild any completed object which had, for example, lead filled silver mounts. When gilding, which would normally be the last operation in making a piece of silver or electroplate, was carried out on fused plate it had to be done before any such mounts were added. Because of this the interesting effect is often produced of having silver mounts on a gilded surface.

Marks

When marks are present they can be helpful. There are three periods in the history of marking of Old Sheffield plate. The first was from about 1755 up to 1773. During this period what are usually described as simulated silver marks were used (No. 11), and many pieces were marked. Today when pieces bearing these marks are found it is usually obvious, with both our knowledge of marks and the objects themselves generally bleeding, that they cannot be silver. In the eighteenth century, however, when new, many such pieces were sold by unscrupulous dealers to unsuspecting

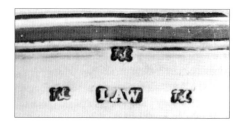

11. Simulated silver marks of Thomas Law, used from 1758 to 1773.

12. Mark of Daniel Holy, Wilkinson & Co., used from 1784 to 1804.

13. Journeymen's marks.

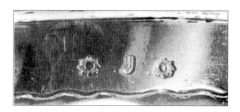

14. Matthew Boulton's sunburst mark used from 1784.

people as silver. Resulting from this petitions were made to Parliament and the marking of Old Sheffield plate was made illegal in 1773.

This second period, of no marks, lasted until 1784, when another Act made it compulsory for all makers, wherever they were working, to register a new mark in Sheffield. By this Act these new marks had in no way to resemble any silver marks, the character of marking favoured being a symbol together with the manufacturer's name in full (No. 12).

Only a few makers appear to have regularly marked their pieces during this third period. Mostly all that will be found are journeymen's marks (No. 13), stamped on pieces to indicate which particular workman within the factory had made them. Pattern numbers referring to the maker's pattern books will also be found quite frequently and are sometimes mistaken for dates, especially when in the 1750-1850 range.

There was an attempt in the 1780s by Matthew Boulton to get marks registered in Birmingham as well as Sheffield. This was one of the few ventures in which he failed. Boulton was, however, one of the only makers during the third period regularly to mark his work. His famous sunburst (No. 14) will be found on the finest pieces of Old Sheffield plate ever produced. A sense of humour seems to have prevailed with this mark where, with later pieces, a face will be found in the centre of the sunburst.

It should be remembered that when, in the 1840s, manufacturers started to produce electroplate, some continued to use the marks which they had been stamping on Old Sheffield plate.

The 1840s were sad years for Old Sheffield plate, with the introduction of the much more economic process of electroplating by Elkingtons. Manufacturers tried to compete by cutting down the thickness of silver on the plate itself and on the mounts. All was in vain; eventually they either had to turn to electroplating or go out of business. The only ones to compete successfully were the button makers who continued to use fused plate until about 1900, fifty years after the main production had effectively ceased.

Re-plating

A question often asked is whether or not Old Sheffield plate should be re-plated. The answer depends very much on the condition of any object. If in good original condition with a desirable amount of bleeding, then it obviously would be vandalism to do so. On the other hand if worn, with large areas of copper exposed, then its beauty and value will have been destroyed. Re-plating will not then restore the piece's value, which has already been lost by virtue of its condition, but it will restore it to something of its original beauty and is in most cases, if well done, acceptable. The exceptions would be pieces of academic interest exhibiting rare or unusual forms of construction.

Since it is impossible to re-Old Sheffield plate, pieces can only be re-plated by electroplating. Resulting from this there are several ways in which it is possible to detect re-plated pieces. The seams, tinning and silver shields will usually be covered, although skilled electroplaters can take measures to protect all but the former. Thus their presence (tinning and shields) is no guarantee that the piece has not been re-plated.

Exposed lead filling on worn silver mounts will not easily electroplate. Therefore, if lead is exposed and yet there are no signs of bleeding on the fused plate, the piece will almost certainly have been re-plated.

Colour is also important. It is only possible to deposit 'pure' silver by electroplating. This is much whiter than the sterling standard silver of fused plate. Look particularly at parts which are difficult to polish; a dead milky white surface here will indicate re-plating. Electroplated objects will also tarnish much more rapidly than fused plate or silver.

There are no short cuts to an ability to recognise Old Sheffield plate. A thorough knowledge of all the methods used in its

construction is the only sure way of making an accurate identification of any objects made using this remarkable form of plating.

ELECTROPLATING

Although there had been earlier experiments and patents for the plating of one metal with another using an electrolytic process, it was Elkingtons' patent of 1840 for the plating of either silver or gold on to another metal that was the effective beginning of a huge new industry.

The method employed was to first make an object in a base metal. At various times copper, nickel, German metal (also known confusingly as nickel silver) which is a cupro-nickel alloy, brass, Britannia metal, gilding metals, steel (indirectly) and others have all been plated using this technique.

Having made the object and prepared its surface (it had to be dirt, grease and blemish free), it is attached to a wire (capable of conducting electricity) and lowered into a plating tank. This tank principally contains a silver salt (e.g. silver cyanide) dissolved in distilled water together with a plate of pure silver suspended by an electricity conducting wire. A low voltage direct current is then switched on, the current flowing from the silver plate through the solution to the object being plated.

As soon as the current is switched on it is as though the object being plated becomes a magnet, drawing silver to it out of the solution (it doesn't actually become a magnet but it is not a bad way of thinking of it). This of course starves the solution of silver. To compensate for this silver goes into solution from the pure silver plate maintaining the balance and eventually 'dissolving' away the silver plate, which then has to be replaced.

When the object is taken out of the plating vat it is a milky white colour and has a dead or fine matt surface. It then has to be polished.

Since the object is made before it is plated casting may be used without problem. The makers also, unlike the Old Sheffield platers, did not have to worry about such things as excess solder since this could be simply rubbed down

163

15. *Example of an Elkington & Co. electroplate mark of 1902.*

16. *Electroplate marks of Henry Wilkinson & Co. with pattern number 6646 and journeyman's initials T.H.*

and plated over. In fact nowhere near the degree of skill, time and effort was required to produce electroplated objects as their equivalent in Old Sheffield plate. Not surprisingly the cheaper – and quite inferior – product electroplate had taken over by the 1850s.

It is perhaps worth considering for a moment why fused or Old Sheffield plate is so much better and lasts so much longer than electroplate. With Old Sheffield the silver is sterling standard which is 'tough' and durable. When electroplating only pure silver can be deposited – this is much softer.

With Old Sheffield the silver is melted on, giving a solid surface; with electroplating a porous and therefore much softer surface is deposited.

With Old Sheffield a toughening known as work hardening takes place with both the production of the sheet and the subsequent making of the object. Since the deposition of the silver on the surface is done after the piece has been made with electroplate, there can be no work hardening.

Burnishing was the standard finishing process with Old Sheffield. This produced in the final stages a very hard surface layer. Although the best electroplate will in the past have been burnished the vast majority will have been polished using a machine, which will not only have no hardening effect, but will also remove quite a bit of the recently deposited silver from the surface.

It is then hardly surprising that two hundred year old pieces of Old Sheffield plate may be found today with their original surface silver, where much electroplate, with similar use, will often require re-plating after only twenty or thirty years – and with some a lot less!

Having said this, there is good quality electroplate to be found, although even this can never equal Old Sheffield.

The best is plated slowly with the object being re-positioned at different angles in the tank three times. This is what is meant by triple plate (it has nothing to do with the thickness of the deposit and does not mean that it is three times as thick!).

The thickness of the deposit is of course important but only has real meaning when taken in conjunction with the speed at which the deposit was formed – the faster it goes on, the faster it comes off!

Thus an object stamped A1 (which refers to a minimum of 25 microns of silver deposited) could be good if slowly, carefully and properly triple plated, or could be very poor and last little time if plated at speed without re-positioning in the tank. Really good electroplate will have in excess of 40 microns triple plated silver on the surface.

Marks

The laws introduced in the eighteenth century preventing Old Sheffield platers from using marks resembling silver marks did not apply to electroplate. Not surprisingly, therefore, the majority of electroplate marks give the visual impression of a set of silver marks.

In an attempt to eliminate this problem a law in the late nineteenth century introduced the legal requirement to use the letters EP. It is clear, however, that many makers, particularly when plating on copper, took a rather cavalier attitude to this law.

EPNS – These letters will often be heavily

disguised. They stand for Electro Plated Nickel Silver and not, as I once heard, for 'Extra Particularly Nice Silver'!

ELECTROPLATED BRITANNIA METAL
EPBM provided the cheapest of the nineteenth century silver look-alikes. Britannia metal itself was a pewter-like alloy developed in the late eighteenth century and known originally as 'White Metal'. It consisted mainly of tin to which small quantities of antimony and a little copper were added.

It was particularly in the second half of the nineteenth century that Britannia metal was electroplated. The most prolific producer was Dixons.

Identifying pieces is quite easy. Most are marked EPBM. When the plate wears through the pewter-like colour of the metal should be clear. If you are at all in doubt tap the piece; if it is EPBM it will have a dull 'thud' rather than a hard metallic ring.

Pitfalls
When worn or damaged it can rarely be satisfactorily either re-plated or repaired. It will also (unless a collectors' market develops for EPBM) be uneconomic to do so. The cost of repairing a piece will normally be far greater than the value of a similar object in fine condition.

Keep Britannia metal away from any heat, for example oven hotplates or Agas. It is surprising how quickly (and expensively for your oven) the piece will melt!

ELECTROPLATE ON STEEL
As with close plate it is not possible to electroplate silver directly on to steel. By the late nineteenth century the problem was overcome by plating the steel first with nickel, then with copper and finally with silver.

The blades and prongs of dessert and fish eaters are the examples most commonly found. Identification is usually easy
- most are marked EP.
- a magnet will stick (as with close plate).
- when worn the colours of the other metals show through quite distinctly.

ELECTROFORMING/ELECTROTYPES
Developed by Elkingtons in the mid-nineteenth century this is a method by which a piece could be grown in a mould. Most often this is done in copper (which is then electroplated over in silver); more unusually a piece would be grown completely in silver.

The technique is to take a moulding of an existing object. This would either be made specifically with this in mind (Elkington Editions are a good example) or it may be an important early piece. (All the Elizabethan silver in the Kremlin, for example, had mouldings taken and electrotypes made in the late Victorian period.)

The mould is made of a special rubber which will conduct electricity and can be peeled off the object which has grown in or on it.

Having made the mould and protected any surfaces not to be 'plated', it is then wired and placed in an electroplating vat in the normal way (see above). As the current is passed through copper or silver is deposited on the mould. This is left to 'grow' until a thick enough 'body' has formed.

When ready the mould is peeled off and a perfect copy of the original should have been produced on the side facing the mould. The other side, however, will be very rough and uneven (almost coral like). This is a distinctive feature of electroformed objects. In many cases, the rough surface is covered to hide it. Electroformed boxes/caskets for example are usually lined with material or wood whereas the bowls of cups most often have a metal lining inserted.

Pitfalls
Occasionally, when taking a moulding from an early piece, the hallmarks were also copied. When this has happened the piece will actually contravene the Hallmarking Laws. (Any such piece should be sent to the Assay Master at the Goldsmiths' Hall in London.)

Electroformed objects are quite brittle and should be handled with extra care since any cracks are virtually impossible to restore.

CHAPTER 15

Fakes, Forgeries and Alterations

British silver is the safest area of the arts as regards forgery and alteration. The reason for this is that the laws governing silver are, and have been, so strict (and for the most part so strictly enforced) that few have risked falling foul of them.

Today a prison sentence of up to ten years awaits anyone found guilty of forging a hallmark or removing a genuine hallmark from one piece and putting it on to another. No other art is so well protected.

The reason for the severity of the law is all to do with the coinage. In the past if people put forged marks or transposed (cut out from one piece and put on to another) genuine marks on to a piece of sub-standard silver (below 92.5%) a very serious problem could arise. This was that the Mint would readily accept hallmarked wares, without testing their purity, for immediate conversion into coinage. If base metal was accepted in this way it would of course debase the coinage and lead to serious economic problems. Forgery or transposition of hallmarks was therefore put on a par with the forgery of coins and banknotes.

1. Scattered marks on a correctly marked piece of 1734 (London) silver. Sotheby's

Despite the severity of the law there have, and probably always will be, those willing to risk the penalties for their own gain. Broadly there are two groups of illegalities that may be found – 'Antique' and 'Modern'.

'Antique' forgeries may be divided between attempts to pass off base metal as silver and tax evasion or duty dodging.

The former is so rarely encountered today (most examples having long since been detected) that it presents very little danger. The latter, known as 'Duty Dodgers', do regularly appear on the market and therefore require explanation and some pointers to their detection.

Duty dodgers first appear in about 1720 as a direct result of a tax (sixpence per ounce) being imposed on silver. The goldsmiths were not at all happy about this and several started to evade the tax.

A small piece (such as a salt or small salver, inexpensive to make and costing little to have hallmarked and taxed) would be produced. The marks would then be cut out and soldered on to a larger piece such as a coffee pot, kettle or two-handled cup.

The problem today is that you will encounter a piece which, on dating stylistically, you decide is, for example, c.1730 and on examining the marks you find has hallmarks of 1728. Everything appears to add up and indeed this will be a perfectly genuine piece of that date and yet it is as illegal a piece today as when the marks were soldered in in 1728.

Taking coffee and teapots as our first examples (since these are the duty dodgers most likely to be encountered), how can you tell?

Look at the positioning of the marks underneath the coffee/tea pot. When genuinely marked as a tea/coffee pot the marks were 'scattered' around the centre (No 1). If the marks appear in a line (No. 2) then the source will have been a small salver and the piece, if

2. Transposed marks in a straight line on the base of a duty dodger. Goldsmiths' Company

eighteenth century, will be a duty dodger (this assumes it is not a more modern forgery). Coffee pots hallmarked next to the top handle socket are safe from duty dodging.

Pieces such as cups, casters and sauceboats present a different problem. With these the plate bearing the marks would be soldered on to the base of the pieces at the same time as the foot, giving a double 'skin' at this point. (Nos. 3 and 4)

If you were able to measure the thickness of the body this would reveal the extra thickness at this point. However, without very special instruments this is not possible, but there is a clue. Look inside for the 'ghost' marks which

are always formed when a piece is hallmarked. If these are not present you may well have a duty dodger. Do remember, though, that where they might show (e.g. on sauceboats), 'ghost' marks would be removed during the final finishing.

When a duty dodger is detected today it is brought within the law by having its hallmarks cancelled (crossed out) and is struck with a London Assay Office punch together with its Antiques Plate Committee Case number (see below). It may then be sold legally. The usual description in a sale catalogue would refer to it as being 'An 18th century ... bearing the cancelled marks for 17—.

Modern forgery is something quite different. It is largely based on the prices paid today for antique silver and in particular for certain makers or types of object.

Examples range from the ridiculous (a George III cocktail shaker and cigarette lighter by Paul Storr springs to mind) to the extremely clever and well researched. Fortunately most fall somewhere between these two.

There are for the most part no quick and easy answers to detecting modern forgeries – experience and knowledge is what really counts here. Help is however at hand. If you are at all suspicious of a piece then you may submit it to the Antiques Plate Committee of the Worshipful Company of Goldsmiths in the City of London.

They use not only their own expertise but, where necessary, have the back-up of various scientific tests to decide whether in their opinion a piece is genuine or not.

3. Duty dodger of about 1730 (see No. 4 for base with foot removed. Goldsmiths' Company

4. Cup in No. 3 with foot removed showing additional plate with transposed hallmarks.
Goldsmiths' Company

5. *Lyons and Twynam forged hallmarks. Note the distinctive shape of the leopard's head punch.*
Goldsmiths' Company

6. *Cast forgeries, in this case wall sconces, showing identical positioning, angles, depth, etc., of marks on each.* Goldsmiths' Company

The most famous forgery case was that of Lyons and Twynam in the late nineteenth century. Suspicions were aroused and an inspection was carried out of the stock of Ruben Lyons shop in Holborn. Nearly all his stock of over three hundred pieces was found to be forgeries.

It was clear that he was not the maker of these but Lyons would not reveal his source. Investigations were carried out and in 1899 Charles Twynam's premises were searched. There nearly one thousand pieces were found along with some thirty-six forged hallmark punches.

Fortunately Lyons & Twynam's knowledge of both antique silver and hallmarks was somewhat limited and as a result many mistakes were made by them. The most usual is to find that the 'date' of the hallmarks does not agree with the design of the piece. With the marks always examine particularly the crowned leopard's head. The punch most often used for this by Lyons & Twynam has a very odd and distinct shape to it (No. 5). It is as though its base has been filed off at an angle. This is so distinctive that the forgers may just have well signed their work.

It would be fascinating to know just how many forgeries Lyons and Twynam put on to the market before they were imprisoned. Judging by the fact that today, some hundred years later, their forgeries are the ones that you are most likely to come across, it must have been many thousands.

When a forgery is detected the piece is brought within the law by having the marks removed. After this it may be modern

hallmarked (if up to standard). As with duty dodgers, an Antiques Plate Committee Case Number will be stamped on the piece.

Casting (see page 33) has often been used as a technique by forgers to produce, in particular, candlesticks and early spoons.

The forger simply uses a genuine example as his casting pattern. An exact copy of the original, including the marks, is then produced.

When a pair or more are found detection is usually easy if you line the marks up. On genuine pieces there will be variations, sometimes slight, in the order, position and angles of the marks on each piece. With cast forgeries the marks will be identical in all respects on each piece (see No. 6). So always remember that up to the middle of the eighteenth century each punch was struck individually by hand on each piece.

Obviously the above method of detection cannot be used for individual examples but since most forgers are motivated by money they tend to try selling sets, which are more valuable, rather than individual pieces.

Alterations

This is the problem you are most likely to meet. Alterations vary from the practical (the most common) where someone has converted a piece they no longer have a use for into something they do (usually destroying the value of the piece in the process), to the

8. George III sugar converted into a 'rare' bachelor teapot.   Goldsmiths' Company

7. An 18th century tankard converted in the 19th century into a coffee pot.   Goldsmiths' Company

fraudulent, where a deliberate attempt has been made to alter the piece in such a way as to enhance its value.

The usual examples are conversion from mugs and tankards into jugs and coffee pots (No. 7). Most of these were carried out in the nineteenth century, although I do still meet people who have converted their christening mugs into cream jugs.

What few realise is that it is illegal to do this without having first obtained the permission of an authorised Assay Office. Having obtained this and carried out the alteration the piece will then have the new parts marked (with additional marks). If, however, the piece has been so radically altered that its character is changed, the law then requires it to be marked as a new ware.

Having said what the law requires, the reality is that you will find that the majority of such pieces have been altered without submission to an Assay Office and as such contravene the hallmarking laws. Should you suspect that you have such a piece then it should be sent to the Antiques Plate Committee at Goldsmiths' Hall where, if necessary, it will be brought within the law.

As mentioned above, most alterations were carried out in the past to make something

useful out of an unwanted or obsolete object. More recently fraudulent alterations have been carried out to deliberately enhance the value of a piece. The following examples will give some idea of what may be found.

The above bachelor teapot (No. 8) from the early nineteenth century, were it genuine, would be a rare and consequently more desirable and valuable piece than the sugar basin from which it has been made. A useful clue here is that the marks are on the side – perfectly acceptable for a sugar basin of this date but certainly not for a teapot.

Unlike the usual conversion from tankard to coffee pot by the simple expedient of adding a spout and insulating the handle (No. 7), with No. 10 someone has gone to a great deal of trouble. They have also, fortunately, made a number of mistakes.

Notice that the lid has a thumb piece and no finial. This you would find on a tankard but never on a coffee pot. (Note: some early coffee pots do have both a thumb piece and a finial.)

The position of the marks is also wrong. What has happened here is that in order to obtain the correct proportion for a coffee pot the height has been increased leaving the marks in a much lower position than they should be (compare with No. 9 which is genuine).

A further mistake (well worth remembering) is that this coffee pot has a fully marked lid. This is fine for tankards of this period but not for a coffee pot which should have only a partially marked lid.

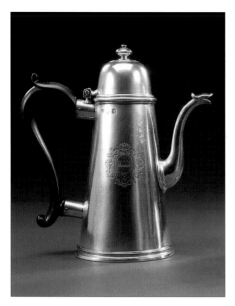

9. Genuine George I coffee pot.   Sotheby's

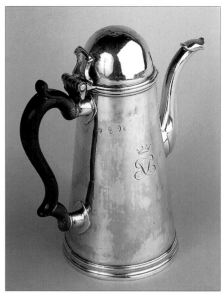

10. Fraudulent alteration of a George I tankard into a coffee pot.   Goldsmiths' Company

Many an odd eighteenth century plate has had its comparatively low value enhanced by altering it into a much more desirable 'strawberry dish'. Two things usually give the game away here – the marks are generally stretched (No. 11) through the re-shaping and the piece as a whole tends to have rather 'thin and whippy' edges.

The above examples all break the law and cannot be legally sold. A more difficult area is that of decoration, in particular engraving and sometimes flat chasing.

For many years the unscrupulous have enhanced the value of pieces by adding interesting armorials and inscriptions. (It is, for example, amazing what the arms of Admiral Lord Nelson will do to the value of a piece).

Sometimes it is the decoration itself which will greatly enhance the value. The flat chased chinoiseries of the 1680s can make an enormous difference. Sadly, as a result there are now pieces which had been perfectly respectable plain 1680s pieces of silver until

recently but which now sport 'desirable' chinoiserie flat chasing.

With both the above types of 'enhancement' the hallmarking laws are unfortunately unable to help since in neither case would they be broken. A good and genuine provenance is always helpful and, not surprisingly, auction houses are putting increasing emphasis on this.

11. Stretched marks resulting from re-shaping after hallmarking.   Goldsmiths' Company

CHAPTER 16

How to Buy

First and foremost buy a piece because you like it. Having decided that you like it, or even gone so far as to have fallen in love with it (can be dangerous!), then the following checklist should help.

1. *Quality* (see page 172). Is it the best for that type of object?
2. *Condition.* Is it worn? Are there any repairs? Does it require restoration work?
3. *Maker.* How good is he/she? Are you paying extra for a fashionable name?
4. *Marks.* Always a tricky one. I would always have a superb piece with badly struck or maker's mark only in preference to a worn out piece with superb marks. Are you paying a premium for a rare mark? If this does not interest you then is there any point in paying the extra?

I often find when a collector starts that there is a tendency in that initial fit of enthusiasm to rush around purchasing just about anything.

Do try to curb this. The best collections always have quality not quantity – one superb piece is far better than half a dozen mediocre or poor examples.

Try to do a bit of research before you embark on collecting a particular type of object. Are they available in sufficient quantity and variety that you will be able to acquire them and form an interesting collection?

In addition, and very importantly, are you able to afford the very best of what you would like to collect? If the answer is 'no' then think again. There is nothing more frustrating than finding that the pieces you would really love are always just out of reach. It is far better to choose an area where you will always be able to afford the very finest examples.

By all means look around but it is not a bad idea to find a dealer in whom you have confidence and who understands your area of collecting and let him help you.

The best advice as to who to choose is to talk to a few. Are they really interested? Do they really have a good enough depth of knowledge to advise you properly? Important dealers do not attach so much importance to smaller pieces whereas for dealers in, say, a street market the item may be the most important piece to have passed through their hands.

It is a mistake to ask a lot of dealers to look for a specific type of object for you. You may well find that you have created an artificial demand – thus pushing up the price you will have to pay! You may in effect end up bidding against yourself!

Auctions

To the uninitiated these are often a daunting prospect. However, once you know the basic principles they can be a good source.

Always examine very carefully any lot you wish to bid for. It is up to you to satisfy yourself as to condition, repairs, originality of engraved armorials, etc. Some auctioneers will give good reliable condition reports if asked (generally those that have a good specialist department), but many do not or cannot be relied on simply because they do not have the required expertise.

It is always worth considering the option of commissioning a good specialist dealer to give you a report on any lot and to bid on your behalf. You are then far less likely to end up with a bad purchase.

If you do decide to bid on your own account then a few guide lines may be of some help. Always decide in advance your top bid, and remember that there will normally be a buyers' premium of usually between 10% and 15% plus VAT on the premium. (For some lots there may be VAT on the whole purchase price – such lots should be marked accordingly in the catalogue.)

You should also decide in advance what to do if you are 'wrong footed' in your bidding. It is not always possible to join the bidding at the right point. If, for example, you have decided to bid up to £200 you may find that having yourself bid £180 your opponent then bids the £200 which was your limit and leaves you with the option of dropping out or going to the next bid which may be £220. (Some auctioneers accept a smaller increment than their norm – it may be worth a try.)

If you are unfamiliar with a particular auctioneer it is a very good idea to arrive in good time to get used to his style and, importantly, the increments he uses in various price ranges.

Many of the top auctioneers require you to register before you bid and will provide you with a bidding number. (This saves names having to be called out and helps to speed up the bidding.) To bid most people simply attract the auctioneer's attention by looking at him and holding up their catalogue. Only two people bid against each other at any one time so don't take it personally if he appears to ignore you and carries on bidding elsewhere. Once one of those already bidding drops out he will then look for a new bidder.

Many people are very worried that if they just scratch their nose they will find themselves the owner of a moth-eaten stag's head. As will be seen from the above, it really doesn't work like that. If, however, a mistake is made (we are all human, after all) and a lot has been knocked down to you which you were not bidding on, or the auctioneer has failed to see and take your bid and has knocked it down to someone else, then say so immediately. A good auctioneer should then put the lot up again.

Always remember that at auction it is the principle of 'let the buyer beware'. Only if a piece is subsequently proved to fall outside the law (see Chapter 15) are you likely to get your money back.

Markets

The range is enormous. At the bottom end is a stall in a general street market or car boot sale. It is probably best if your knowledge is limited to buy only pieces you like at a price you feel it is worth to you (regardless of its real value).

At the top end (and usually under cover!) are some very good and often well established specialist dealers who can be very knowledgeable and helpful in their particular field. You will probably pay the going rate but most collectors soon realise that bargain hunting is no way to form a fine collection.

In between are an extraordinary variety of dealers from remarkably divergent backgrounds.

Fairs

As with markets, the range is enormous. At the bottom end many call themselves 'Fairs' but they are really only market stalls under cover (see Markets above).

The better fairs – those I would regard as the true 'Antique Fairs', following in the tradition of the Grosvenor House Fair – have strict guide lines as to date, acceptable degrees of restoration, etc., and will have vetting of all pieces.

Vetting does vary. At best it is carried out by independent experts (i.e. those not exhibiting) who will normally be named. Vetting by a team of the exhibitors themselves, which does happen at many fairs, does not perhaps instil the same degree of confidence.

Prices at such fairs are often high – particularly on the first day. They are, however, often a good way of meeting and getting to know dealers from parts of the country you may not normally visit.

Quality

This may be broken down into three principal areas: design, workmanship and condition.

Design

Any object should first and foremost fulfil the function for which it is intended. Taking for example a coffee pot, does it produce a good cup of coffee? Does it feel comfortable in the hand? Does it pour without dripping or, even worse, 'glugging'? Is the spout set sufficiently high so that the dregs remain in the pot and are not flushed out with the coffee? (I am always amazed at how few people actually try a piece before they buy it.) All are important questions but how often are they addressed when a pot is being purchased.

After function then aesthetics. Is it well proportioned? If there is any decoration how well does this, as well as heraldic devices, initials, inscriptions etc., harmonise with the overall form, and is it contemporary with the piece?

Workmanship

How is the piece made? (see Chapter 4). Has the maker used a good thickness of metal or not? Does the piece feel nice and 'chunky' or rather light and flimsy? Don't be afraid to pick pieces up. You will be surprised how quickly you get a feel for when a piece is 'just right' (chunky without being too heavy) – only practical experience will do here.

Condition

A piece may be beautifully designed and superbly made but all is lost if it has had a hard life. A number of questions should be asked.

Is there any damage and if so is it easily restorable without adverse effect on the piece? Are there any old repairs?
How crisp is the piece and any decoration engraving etc. on it?
How good is the patina?
Are all the decorative elements present contemporary with the piece?
Are any arms/crests/initials/inscriptions contemporary?

Damage

Dents are in most cases comparatively easy for a restorer to deal with. There are however exceptions, particularly when a dent is in a difficult place to reach. Amongst the most problematic, and consequently expensive, are loaded candlesticks (see page 56). The restorer in most cases has to take these to pieces before the dent can be removed and then of course has to reassemble the stick!

Splits are a far more serious problem since soldering is required which can affect the colour/patination of the piece (particularly if done badly – unfortunately so often the case).

Old repairs. If you can see these easily then they are in most cases a serious problem. Always remember that it is generally very difficult if not impossible for a restorer to deal with an old botched repair.

How *crisp* is the piece? Look particularly at the edges and the high points.

Colour/Patination

The surface or skin of any piece is of great importance and is a combination of two factors – colour and patination.

Although pure silver is a white metal the silver used in the making of any object has, as we have already seen (page 11), copper added to it. This not only makes it more durable but the small amount involved subtly changes its colour.

If you put a piece of British Sterling (925) standard next to one of German 800 standard you should notice the slightly 'greyer' colour of the latter.

With antique silver there is, however, another very important influence on colour known as fire or fire skin. It is this that gives that wonderful 'blue/grey' colour to antique silver in fine condition.

Fire results from the annealing process (page 31). During this, the copper present in the alloy at the surface oxidises at red heat. The longer and more often the piece is red hot the greater will be the depth of this skin.

It is easiest to see this if you look underneath many eighteenth century pieces where the assay scrape remains (salvers are usually particularly good for this). The white patch is where the sample for assay has been taken. In doing this it cuts through the fire skin revealing the true, whiter colour of the silver underneath.

From the mid/late nineteenth century onwards manufacturers have increasingly tried to get rid of or to avoid this fire. Today much of what is made in silver is actually electroplated to cover what are generally, as a result of modern soldering techniques, very patchy fire skins. When the plating wears off these pieces the results are awful. It is an extraordinary thought that much modern manufactured silver may in the future have to

Broken Fire

be electroplated periodically to cover again these bad surfaces. This in turn means that such pieces may never acquire a fine patina.

With polishing and use the fire skin slowly wears away until the silver is entirely white. The intermediate stage often gives a mottled or sometimes rather patchy surface. This is referred to as broken fire. Obviously the less the fire is broken the better. Few antique pieces have a perfect fire skin; very many have no fire skin left at all.

As with furniture, so with silver – the surface of any piece develops with age. While this is comparatively easy to see on furniture, the highly reflective surface of silver makes it more difficult. Practice and experience is the only real answer here. A suggestion would be to buy, from a dealer who knows and understands, a really fine eighteenth century table spoon (even the best are not expensive) with a very fine patina and use this for comparison.

Patina itself is a combination of fire skin and the ageing of the surface. With the latter fine scratches inevitably occur when any piece is used. In turn these are gradually 'softened' with repeated polishing and handling. Too much wear and tear or over-polishing and a poor patina will result. A fine patina is a great asset.

CHAPTER 17

Care, Cleaning and Conservation

The question I am asked probably more than any other is 'How should I look after my silver?' It is a very important question since a great deal of the damage to be found on antique silver today results not from careless use but from mistakes made during the cleaning and polishing process This is sad since this damage would have been entirely avoidable if only the correct techniques had been used.

Before looking at the techniques it is important to consider what it is that actually makes silver tarnish or acquire green or black spots. Armed with this knowledge it is often possible to prevent or at least reduce some of the problems.

Two substances, sulphur and chlorine, cause most of the problems, It is the sulphur in the atmosphere that tarnishes silver This is a comparatively new problem resulting from the thousands of tons of sulphur emitted by industry. Prior to the Industrial Revolution it would have been possible to leave silver exposed to the atmosphere for long periods with little or no tarnishing. Other than campaigning to curb sulphur emissions there is little that can be done to prevent silver from tarnishing as a result of this 'background' atmospheric sulphur.

There are however, domestic sources of sulphur which can increase the rate at which our silver tarnishes. A little thought and common sense here can make a significant difference. The most obvious is an open fire burning ordinary household coal. Any silver in close proximity to this will tarnish more rapidly. Less obvious would be oil-fired boilers/stoves, etc., around which sulphur levels will be increased. Here the problem arises not with display but with silver that has been stored nearby. With both of the above sensible relocation is advisable.

A surprising but normally short term problem can arise as a result of acquiring a new wool carpet. Wool contains sulphur which is given off in significant quantities when new. The result of course is that any silver in the room will tarnish much faster. For the same reason materials either made of wool or with a wool content should never be used for silver storage or display.

What of the second problem – chlorine? This attacks silver in one of two ways. The first is where it is combined with sodium (sodium chloride) to form salt. If simple rules are followed when using salt there should be no problem. Filling the salt-cellars should be one of the last things when setting a table. It is not a bad idea to work on the principle that when you light the candles you fill the salts. Then, after the main course, the salts should be removed, emptied, rinsed and dried. If a glass liner is present this must never be left in the salt-cellar with salt in it.

Glass liners were only introduced in the mid-eighteenth century as a result of the development of pierced salt-cellars at that time. Unfortunately, during the nineteenth century they started to be fitted to salts which never originally had them. People then, thinking they had solved the problem, left them with the salt in. What happens is that grains of salt inevitably fall into the space between the glass and the silver. Verdigris (see below) then forms and permanent damage is done. Do not use a glass liner unless it is absolutely necessary.

A further important point is that salt must never be left in the same cupboard, box, etc., as silver. It may seem safe with silver on the top shelf and salt on the bottom, but it is not. Microscopic particles of salt will be lifted by the air currents when the doors are opened and closed. These will eventually settle on the silver setting off verdigris.

Many salts have their interiors gilded to protect the silver. The same rules as above apply, since although gilding gives far better protection it is not 100 per cent. There are two reasons for this. First, salt grains will be deposited on the unprotected exterior however careful you may be and, secondly, with use tiny areas of silver will eventually be exposed as the gilding wears away.

The second way in which chlorine may affect silver is rather insidious. This is through tap water. All mains supplies have chlorine added. For this reason how silver is washed is very important. Silver that is in regular use and properly washed and dried should retain a good polish and require little other attention.

Never put silver into a dish washer. Silver must always be hand washed and should always be the first to be washed. This is because the longer silver is left the more tarnish will form where traces of various vegetables (sprouts, peas, etc., all contain sulphur) together with egg (high in sulphur) and, of course, salt remain in contact. The longer any of these are left the more work you will eventually have to do.

What of the washing-up itself? Most standard washing-up liquids are safe to use so long as thorough rinsing is carried out afterwards (most washing-up liquid contains salt) but avoid anything with an added fragrance, e.g. lemon. Do not throw all the spoons and forks in together as this will result in surface damage as pieces rub against each other. As each piece is washed it should after rinsing either be handed to the person drying, or, if working alone, be placed in a bowl of warm water (except knives – see below) ready to be dried later. Silver should never be left to 'drip dry' since this concentrates any chlorine present. The resulting surface damage will not be immediately obvious as it builds up slowly with each successive wash.

Old knives usually have pitch-filled handles and for this reason they should always be held with the blade only in the water. The handle itself should then be cleaned separately. When putting knives down always make sure that they are all faced in the same direction. If this is not done then irreparable damage may easily be done to the handles by the blades.

Rubber gloves should never be worn when working with silver. If a wet or messy process is being carried out then plastic surgical/disposable or plastic-coated cotton gloves may be used. If dry, then use cotton gloves. Contact with other rubber should always be avoided. This is because sulphur is introduced during the vulcanising process, and this, unlike ordinary sulphur tarnish, forms a permanent bond with silver. The only way the resulting black stain can be removed is literally to rub it away. This removes a significant amount of silver and does permanent damage. Apart from rubber gloves, pencil rubbers and rubber bands should never be left on or around any piece of silver. Be careful when putting a piece of silver into a drawer. I have seen many a cigarette case with a bad rubber stain where it has almost certainly been in contact with some knicker elastic!

One final problem before looking at actual cleaning techniques. I have on a number of occasions been approached for advice on 'little black spots' that have mysteriously appeared on the dining-table silver. The usual cause of this is the zest from an orange or the juice from a lemon or grapefruit – which sets off the formation of verdigris. It is as well to rinse thoroughly and dry any silver where there is a danger of the above.

Removing Tarnish

Straightforward sulphur tarnish may be tackled in one of two ways. You may either remove the tarnish from the surface or convert it back into silver.

For the removal of tarnish one of two substances may be used – whiting or jeweller's rouge. Basically any polish that is white in colour will be based on whiting, and any (the majority) of a rouge colour will be based on jeweller's rouge. These may be described as the traditional polishes.

Whenever working on any piece of silver two very important rules must always be followed. First, the object must be prepared: any detachable parts must be removed, e.g. teapot finials, candlestick nozzles, candelabra branches and epergne baskets. Second, you must always hold whatever you are working on. You must never

1. Epergnes must always be completely dismantled before cleaning and polishing. A plate brush would be particularly useful here with the arms, legs, borders and the cast openwork decoration between the legs. Phillips

ever work on any piece with it supported in any way on a table top or other hard surface. If it is very large, for instance a tray, then you must work with it on your lap. The reason is quite simple. If you work on a solid surface you will have no idea of how much stress you are applying to the piece. The vast majority of damage to silver results from this mistake. The two most common examples are salvers which are found with a warp and, in extreme cases, with broken feet or splits to the edge of the salver itself, and candlesticks which are frequently found with splits, or repaired splits, at the junction of stem and base.

How a piece is held is important. Always remember that you must support the piece as far as possible in such a way as to avoid stress. If a handle is present this must not be used to hold the piece when polishing. This is a very common mistake and is the cause of so many damaged handle sockets (for wooden handles) or splits to the main body at the junction of the handle with body.

Cleaning and Polishing
With a traditional polish a cotton cloth should be used. Never use a cloth containing any man-made fibres since these will damage the surface.

Having applied a little polish (most people use too much) to the cloth and holding the piece correctly, start to polish in small circles over the surface. This is very important. If you do not do this and polish as most people do, with great sweeps in the same direction, you will end up with bad patination (lines will develop in the direction in which you always polish). When the polish is dry then polish off, again using small circles. If heavy decoration is present (e.g. chasing) then a plate brush should when, and only when, necessary be used to remove polish from the nooks and crannies. Plate brushes should be used sparingly and should never be used on a plain surface. Although a plate brush will become quite black with use it should not be washed since this will take some of the spring out of the bristle.

The other way of dealing with tarnish (converting it back into silver) may be achieved in one of two ways.

First the use of silver dip. Contrary to popular belief this does not 'take the surface off'. However, it must be used only according to the instructions given on the container. It should also only be used on badly tarnished pieces which are either completely made of silver, Old Sheffield plate or electroplate on copper. It should not be used on any gilded surfaces.

When using silver dip the object must always be completely covered with it (if this is not done a patchy surface will result). The

2. Candlesticks suffer greatly from being polished whilst being held on a table top. The usual result is splitting between base and stem   Phillips

3. This claret jug looks as though it would be a great problem to clean with its overlay of foliage. In fact all the leafwork sections and the handle are detachable to facilitate cleaning.

4. Bad cleaning and polishing may result in a poor skin. Notice how patchy the body of this coffee pot is.
Phillips

maximum time (usually two minutes) should *never* be exceeded. If tarnish is still present at the end of the maximum time the piece should be washed and dried thoroughly before another application of dip. This may have to be repeated several times on a very badly tarnished piece. It is important to remember, having completed the conversion of the tarnish black to silver with the dip, that the object will then require polishing.

The second way of converting tarnish back into silver (for objects made completely from silver and with no filling or attachment of other material) is with washing soda and aluminium. Simply place a plate of aluminium in the bottom of a bucket with two or three handfuls (wearing plastic gloves) of washing soda and fill with hot water. Having done this place the

5. With this group all the animals must be unbolted before any attempt is made at cleaning and polishing. A plate brush will prove to be particularly useful with such a piece.
Christie's

6. Nefs must present the ultimate cleaning problem. There are no quick answers to this one, only patience and careful work. (Soft bristle toothbrushes and paint-brushes can be quite useful with such an object). A hair-drier is also useful when a wet process has been used.
Phillips

7. Pearls and mother-of-pearl are actually dissolved away by silver dip, so it should never be used on an object like this.
Phillips

piece of silver in the bucket so that it is in contact with the aluminium and leave for a few minutes. As with dip, the object will require polishing afterwards.

Washing soda is also particularly useful for cleaning the inside of tea and coffee pots. Put a handful of washing soda crystals into the pot and fill with hot water (you may also add a couple of aluminium milk bottle tops if you like). Leave for about half an hour, then empty and wipe out with a cotton cloth. Repeat as necessary until the interior is clean. If green/black spots or areas are present (for instance, inside a salt-cellar) then a different technique must be used. Here the problem is verdigris (always with green spots – sometimes with black spots), which is in fact poisonous. The way to tackle this is to use ordinary household ammonia (usually between 10%-15% strength). This must be treated with

8. Salvers must always be very carefully held when being worked on. Warping, split edges (notice the repair directly under the armorial) and broken feet are all common problems resulting from this not having been done. Sotheby's

great respect, avoiding contact with eyes or skin (plastic gloves are a good idea, as is good ventilation). Open the bottle at arm's length and carefully fill the salt-cellar with ammonia. Leave this to soak for an hour or so. If verdigris is present the solution will turn blue (anything from pale to deep Prussian blue depending on the amount of verdigris present). Following this soaking carefully empty the ammonia, thoroughly rinse and then wipe with a cloth. The process should then be repeated until the ammonia no longer turns blue after an hour or so. Should the problem be in an awkward area, then cotton wool soaked in ammonia may be

used. If black/green spots are on a flat surface then a few drops of ammonia may be put on the affected area (unlike dip, the whole area does not have to be covered).

Having dissolved away the verdigris it will be necessary to repolish the affected area. In this case a lot of elbow grease will be necessary, making sure at the same time that the object is not stressed.

Only ever use small amounts of ammonia at a time, and never attempt to brush or agitate it. If ammonia fails to deal with a black spot or mark, then try silver dip (remembering to cover the entire object with dip). If neither of these work then the black mark will almost certainly have been caused by rubber contact and professional help should be sought.

Fine surface scratches such as are often found on salvers after drinks have been served, or on the backs of spoon bowls, may be dealt with comparatively easily. Use a traditional polish using a lot of elbow grease in small circles over the area affected. Remember of course not to stress any part of the piece whilst doing so.

Personal Safety
When using any chemical process always remember to wear eye protection as well as plastic disposable gloves to protect skin. Always work with good ventilation.

Maintenance
Once a piece is both clean and polished, then by using one of the modern long term polishes it should be easy to maintain. The traditional

9. The insides of tea and coffee pots may be cleaned with washing soda. If the finials are detachable these should always be unscrewed before cleaning. Phillips polishes mentioned above should only be used to sort out problems. Points to watch with long term polish are:

First, not to over polish when finishing off; if you do then much of the tarnish inhibitor which makes it 'long term' will be removed.

Secondly, long term foam polishes are wet processes; common sense should be used with any filled objects (e.g. loaded candlesticks) and pieces with wood attached, such as most coasters.

To check if a piece of silver is really clean or not, either breathe on it heavily or place a sheet of good quality white tissue paper close to the surface. In either case any dirt or tarnish remaining will show up very well as black marks.

Polish should not be used with silver gilt and gold. Wash in soap and water and then rub over with a chamois leather. If stains appear on any modern gilding then good professional help should be sought.

Always remember that other materials forming part of a silver object will also require attention. I am always amazed at how little they normally receive. Wood should always be waxed (a good, pure beeswax only), ivory should be cleaned with almond oil and tortoiseshell should be soaked with olive oil or neatsfoot oil With all three it is best that they are dealt with before the silver itself is polished.

Filigree work is always a problem. If it is badly tarnished then silver dip may be used (see above). However, polishing it requires great care. A very soft plate brush used very gently is the answer. A cloth should never be used. Fine bristle (never nylon) toothbrushes can be very useful in awkward places as can bristle paint-brushes (always cover any metal parts with strong insulating tape).

Special silver polishing cloths intended to remove light tarnish have been available for many years. More recently special polishing mitts have come on to the market which I find much more practical. Apart from giving pieces a quick 'once over' they are a very good idea to use when setting a table.

Storage

If this is done properly then it is possible to put silver away clean and polished and know that it should be in that state when you next want to use it. At its most basic, acid free tissue paper may be used. If well wrapped up in this with a sachet of silica gel crystals to maintain a dry atmosphere, the silver should remain tarnish free for a good time (if the box is reasonably airtight).

Newspaper should never be used either to wrap around silver or as padding between objects. The paper itself is highly acidic, and traditional newsprint will etch itself into the surface of the silver! Chamois leather, although used extensively in the past, has now been shown to be harmful and should not be used for storage. Baize, probably the most traditional and extensively used of all materials for silver storage, has also been shown to be harmful; it also should no longer be used.

The best bags, etc., for storage are those made out of closely woven cotton which has been specially treated chemically to repel any harmful gases. Silver may be kept in these for considerable periods of time before showing any signs of tarnish at all.

Plastic bags are much loved by many but again should not be used. They trap any moisture whilst at the same time allowing harmful gases to pass through unhindered to the silver. I was recently shown a teapot which had been put into a plastic bag with a rubber band around to secure it. The result was a black rubber stain running all the way around the pot!

Various 'capsules' are available which when opened and placed in a box/safe/display cabinet will keep silver tarnish free for about a year. These work well so long as the enclosed area is not constantly opened. Do read any instructions carefully, though, since many of these will, for example, age any paper or turquoise that may be present.

Looked after properly silver is the most rewarding of substances. There is to my mind nothing as satisfying as bringing a neglected piece back to its true glory.

Where to see Silver

One of the most important things for anyone studying or interested in silver is to look at and, if feasible, handle as many pieces as possible.

MUSEUMS
A number of museums house important collections of British silver, notably:

London
Bank of England Museum. Particularly late 17th/early 18thC
British Museum. Prehistoric-early 18thC
London Museum. Particularly 18thC
Somerset House. Soon to house the important Gilbert Collection
Tower of London. The Regalia, other Royal Plate and Regimental Silver
Victoria & Albert Museum. Medieval-Modern
Wellington Museum (Apsley House). Regency

West Country
Barnstaple (Museum of North Devon). Barnstaple silver
Bath (Holburne of Menstrie). Extensive collection of 17th-19thC and early spoons
Bristol City Art Gallery, Bristol silver
Exeter (Royal Albert Memorial). Exeter & West Country silver
Plymouth. Small collection of Plymouth silver

South
Alton (Allen House). Small but important collection of spoons
Southampton Art Gallery. Small general collection

East Anglia
Colchester (Holly Tree Museum). Caddy spoons
Norwich Castle Museum. Small collection of Norwich silver

Midlands
Birmingham City Museum and Art Gallery. Birmingham and general silver
Birmingham (Soho House). Matthew Boulton silver and Old Sheffield plate

Oxford (Ashmolean Museum). Very important collection including Farrer collection of Huguenot silver

North
Leeds (Temple Newsam House). Very important collection
Sheffield (Weston Park Museum). Old Sheffield plate and electroplate
Sheffield (Cutlers Hall). Sheffield silver

North East
Barnard Castle Bowes Museum. General
Hull City Museum. Hull silver
Hull (Trinity House). Hull silver
Newcastle (Laing Art Gallery). Newcastle silver
York Museum. The Lee Collection of York silver
York (Fairfax House). Small but fine collection

North West
Chester (Grosvenor Museum). Chester silver
Manchester City Art Gallery. Very important collection of Huguenot silver
Preston (Harris Museum & Art Gallery). Important collection of card cases

Scotland
Edinburgh (Royal Scottish Museum). General collection
Edinburgh (National Museum of Antiquities of Scotland). Important Scottish silver
Edinburgh (Huntley House). Small collection including some important Edinburgh plate
Glasgow City Museum. Glasgow and general silver
Glasgow (Burrell Collection). Small collection

Wales
Cardiff National Museum. Jackson collection and Jackson collection of spoons – very important

Ireland
Belfast (Ulster Museum). Irish and good general silver
Dublin (National Museum). Irish silver

USA (British and American)
Andover, Massachusetts (Addison Gallery of
American Art)
Baltimore Museum of Art, Maryland
Boston Museum of Fine Arts, Massachusetts
Cambridge, Massachusetts (Fogg Art Museum,
Harvard University)
Chicago (Art Institute of Chicago), Illinois
Cincinnatti Art Museum, Ohio
Cleveland Museum of Art, Ohio
Detroit Institute of Arts, Michigan
Los Angeles County Museum, California
Minneapolis Institute of Arts, Minnesota
New Haven, Connecticut (Yale University Art
Gallery)
New York (Albany Institute of History and Art)
New York (Metropolitan Museum of Art)
Philadelphia Museum of Art, Pennsylvania
Philadelphia (Historical Society of Penn-
sylvania)
Portland Art Museum (Portland, Oregon)
Rhode Island School of Design, Providence
St. Louis City Art Museum, Mississippi
San Francisco, California (M.H. de Young
Memorial Collection)
San Marino, California (Huntington Museum)
Toledo Museum of Art, Ohio
Wandsworth Atheneum (Halford County)
Williamsburg, Virginia (Colonial Williamsburg)
Williamstown, Massachusetts (Clark Art
Institute)
Wilmington, Delaware (Winterthur Museum)
Worcester Art Museum, Massachusetts

Canada
Toronto (Royal Ontario)

HOUSES
Anglesey Abbey (NT), Cambridgeshire
Belton House (NT), Grantham, Lincs
Chatsworth, Bakewell, Derbyshire
Dunham Massey (NT), Cheshire
Ickworth (NT), Bury St Edmunds, Suffolk
Knole House (NT), Sevenoaks, Kent
The Royal Pavilion, Brighton, Sussex
Woburn Abbey, Bedfordshire

CHURCH PLATE
For many years much church silver remained
locked away in various bank vaults and safes.
Now, thanks to a policy instigated by Charles

Oman and supported by The Goldsmiths
Company, Treasuries have been opened in many
of the Cathedrals etc throughout the country. At
present these include:

Bury St Edmunds; Canterbury; Carlisle; St
Mary's Church Heritage Centre, Chichester;
Durham; Gloucester; Guildford; Hereford;
Lincoln; Litchfield; Newark; Norwich; Oxford
(Christchurch); Peterborough; Ripon; St Albans;
St Pauls; Salisbury; Westminster Abbey;
Winchester; York.

In addition the Victoria and Albert Museum has
a very large collection of church plate.

Auction Houses
All the top auctioneers hold regular silver sales.
These are often an opportunity to view items
which in many cases will not be accessible again
for many years.
    Auction catalogues, particularly those of
important or specialist sales, are often well worth
purchasing. In some cases catalogues of
particular sales have become important reference
works in their own right.

Exhibitions
These are always worth looking out for. They
are usually advertised in the press but it is also
not a bad idea to get your name on to the various
museum mailing lists (particularly the Victoria
and Albert) together, of course, with the
Worshipful Company of Goldsmiths who
regularly have exhibitions.

Corporate Collections
Abingdon; Guildford; Kings Lynn; Norwich;
Oxford; Portsmouth

Military
Woolwich Arsenal has become an important
centre housing the collections of various dis-
banded regiments as well as their own pieces.

Collegiate
Many of the Colleges in Oxford and Cambridge
as well as such schools as Eton and Winchester
have important collections. In most cases
viewing is by special arrangement and
appointment only.

CHAPTER 19

Courses, Lectures, etc.

A number of organisations are worth investigating.

Museums will normally have regular programmes of lectures which will often include lectures on various aspects of silver. Get on to the mailing list of your local museums and those national ones (e.g. Victoria and Albert) that you are able and are prepared to travel to.

The Silver Society for the serious collector/ enthusiast/scholar, holds monthly lecture meetings in London, organises visits both in Britain and overseas and publishes a regular journal. Contact: Keith Grant-Peterkin, Secretary, The Silver Society, 22 Orlando Road, London SW4 0LF.

The National Association of Decorative and Fine Arts Societies (NADFAS). There are at present in the region of three hundred societies spread throughout most of the United Kingdom together with an increasing number in Europe and Australia. A society's annual programme includes monthly lectures as well as study groups, visits and tours. There are also various national events. Lectures etc. on silver are included periodically in individual society programmes. (Note: You must be a member or a guest to be able to attend.) For information on your nearest member society contact: NADFAS House, 8 Guilford Street, London WC1N 1DT. Tel No 0171 430 0730. Fax 0171 242 0686.

The National Trust & The National Art Collections Fund. Both have lecture pro-grammes organised particularly by their various branches which will periodically include lectures on silver.

The Auction Houses. Sotheby's and Christie's both have Education Departments which are worth contacting. Bonhams have also become involved in providing lectures and courses.

Antiques Clubs. There are many throughout the country. For an up-to-date list and contact telephone numbers etc. see the latest edition of *Antique Collecting,* the journal of the Antique Collectors' Club, 5 Church Street, Woodbridge, Suffolk IP12 1DS.

The Author. Apart from lecturing regularly to many of the organisations mentioned above, I have a number of on-going silver courses (at present held in Beaconsfield, Henley, Newbury and Woking). Information on these and any other of my lectures may be obtained by contacting me c/o The Antique Collectors' Club at the above address.

Specialist Societies/Clubs etc. 'The Silver Spoon Club' of Great Britain publishes a bi-monthly journal. Contact: Terry & Mary Haines, Glenleigh Park, Sticker, St Austell PL26 7JD. Tel. 01726 65269.

The Caddy Spoon Collectors' Club. Meets three times a year and occasionally publishes a newsletter. Contact: Eric Delieb. Tel. 0181 458 2083.

The Wine Label Circle, 45 Shepherds Hill, London N6 5QJ.

Bibliography

General

The Collectors Dictionary of Silver & Gold
Michael Clayton
Antique Collectors' Club Edition 1985

The Price Guide to Antique Silver
Peter Waldron
Antique Collectors' Club 2nd Edition 1982

The History of Silver
General Editor Claude Blair
Macdonald Orbis 1987

Sotheby's Concise Encyclopedia of Silver
General Editor Charles Truman
Conran Octopus 1993

Silver
G Taylor
Penguin 1956

*Jacksons Silver & Gold Marks of England,
Scotland and Ireland*
Antique Collectors' Club 1989

To carry around

Jackson's Hallmarks (Pocket Edition)
Editor Ian Pickford
Available in hardback or paperback
Antique Collectors' Club

Specific Periods

London: 1697-1837
London Goldsmiths (marks and biographies)
A. Grimwade
Faber & Faber 1976

London: 1838-1914
The Directory of Gold and Silversmiths 2 vols
(marks and biographies)
John Culme
Antique Collectors' Club 1987

Silver in Tudor and Early Stuart England
P. Glanvill
Victoria & Albert Museum 1991

Caroline Silver
C.C. Oman
Faber & Faber 1970

Huguenot Silver in England
J.F. Hayward
Faber & Faber 1959

The Huguenot Legacy
English Silver 1680-1760
Christopher Hartop
Thomas Heneage 1996

Rococo Silver (mid-18th century)
A. Grimwade
Faber & Faber 1974

Adam Silver (late 18th century)
R. Rowe
Faber & Faber 1965

Nineteenth Century Silver
J. Culme
Country Life 1977

Victorian Silver
P. Wardle
Herbert Jenkins 1963

Modern Silver throughout the World
G. Hughes
Studio Vista 1967

Regional Silver

The Silversmiths of Birmingham
General Editor K Crisp Jones
NAG Press 1981

Chester Silver
M. Ridgway
Vol I up to 1726, Vol II 1727-1837
John Sherratt & Son 1968 and 1985
Vol III 1857-1962
Gee & Son 1996

A Directory of Newcastle Goldsmiths
M.A.V. Gill 1976

Norwich Silver
G.N. Barrett
Wensum Press 1981

'Salisbury Silver 1550-1700'
T.A. Kent
The Silver Society Journal No 3
Spring 1993

Scottish Gold and Silver Work
Finlay
New Edition Strong Oak Press 1991
Revised by Henry Stuart Fotheringham

Collecting Irish Silver
D. Bennett
Souvenir Press 1984

Subjects

Silver Spoons
M Snodin
Letts Revised Edition 1982

Silver Flatware 1660-1980
Ian Pickford
Antique Collectors' Club 1983

London Silver Spoonmakers 1500-1679
T.A. Kent
The Silver Society 1981

*West Country Silver Spoons and their Marks
    1550-1750*
T.A. Kent
J.H. Bourdon Smith 1992

The Book of the Wine Label
N.M. Penzer
White Lion Press
Reprint 1974

Hennell Silver Salt Cellars
Percy Hennell
BLA 1986

Caddy Spoons
John Norie
John Murray 1988

Monteith Bowls
G.E. Lee
Manor House Press 1978

History of Old Sheffield Plate
F. Bradbury
Facsimile
Northend 1968

Understanding Silver Plate
Stephen J. Helliwell
Antique Collectors' Club 1996

Makers

*Matthew Boulton and the Toymakers of
    Birmingham*
Goldsmiths Hall Exhibition Catalogue 1982

The Courtauld Silver
J.F. Hayward
Sotheby Parke Bernet 1975

Paul de Lamerie
Goldsmiths Hall Exhibition Catalogue 1990

Paul Storr
N.M. Penzer
Batsford 1954

George Wickes
E. Barr
Studio Vista 1980Abercorn, Dukes of,

Index of Names and Makers

General Index